I0040851

False Claims Act & Qui Tam

Quarterly Review

Volume 83 • January 2017
Edited by Jacklyn DeMar
Taxpayers Against Fraud
TAF Education Fund

Copyright © 2017 TAF Education Fund

All Rights Reserved.

ISBN 978-0-9992185-1-8

Published by
Taxpayers Against Fraud
TAF Education Fund
1220 19th Street NW, Suite 501
Washington, DC 20036
Phone (202) 296-4827
Fax (202) 296-4838

Printed in the United States of America

The *False Claims Act and Qui Tam Quarterly Review* is published by the Taxpayers Against Fraud Education Fund. This publication provides an overview of major False Claims Act and *qui tam* developments including case decisions, DOJ interventions, and settlements.

The TAFEF is a nonprofit charitable organization dedicated to combating fraud against the government through the promotion and use of the *qui tam* provisions of the False Claims Act ("FCA"). The TAFEF serves to inform and educate the general public, the legal community, and other interested groups about the FCA and its *qui tam* provisions.

The TAFEF is based in Washington, D.C., where it maintains a comprehensive FCA library for public use and a staff of lawyers and other professionals who are available to assist anyone interested in the False Claims Act and *qui tam*.

TAF Education Fund

Board of Directors	President's Council	Advisory Committee
Neil Getnick, *Chairman*	Kenneth Nolan, *Chairman*	Michael Behn
James Breen	James Breen	John Clark
T. Mark Jones	Neil Getnick	Erika Kelton
Erika Kelton	Glenn Grossenbacher	Mark Kleiman
Cheryl Meads	James Helmer	Timothy McInnis
John Phillips	Erika Kelton	Rick Morgan
Margaret Richardson	Scott Powell	Lesley Skillen
Shelley Slade	Jennifer Verkamp	Shelley Slade
Linda Sundro	Joseph E.B. White	David Stone

Professional Staff
Robert Patten, *President and Chief Executive Officer*
Patrick Burns, *Associate Director*
Jacklyn DeMar, *Director of Legal Education*
Takeia Kiett, *Director of Membership Services*
Miranda Houchins, *Communications Specialist*
Michael DeJesus, *Public Interest Advocacy Fellow*

Taxpayers Against Fraud Education Fund
1220 19th Street NW
Suite 501
Washington, DC 20036
Phone (202) 296-4826
Fax (202) 296-4838
www.taf.org

TABLE OF CONTENTS

Judgments & Settlements 91

Leatha Henderson

Bechtel National and AECOM

Dr. Anthony Clavo

ManTech International

Mousetrap Pediatrics PC

Zwanger & Pesiri Radiology Group LLP

Niurka Fernandez and Robert Alverez

Dan Horsky

Network Services Solutions

Biocompatibles

Air Industries Corporation

Ormat Technologies, Inc.

Life Care Centers

Hudson Valley Associates, RLLP

K3 Learning, Inc.

Omnicare, Inc.

Five Rochester-area Contractors

Gateway, Inc.

Mylan

Whittier Health Network, Inc.

Burlington Labs Inc. and Burlington Labs LLC

Novartis Pharmaceuticals Corporation

Armor Correctional Health Services

Yavapai Regional Medical Center

Primary Residential Mortgage Inc. and Security National Mortgage
  Company

Three Orthopedic Clinics

Tenet Health Care

FROM THE EDITOR

Taxpayers Against Fraud Education Fund is pleased to bring you a journal article written by our former Public Interest Advocacy Fellow, Laura K. Wilk. The article focuses on grant and research fraud and how best to tackle the thorny issues that often come up in those cases. We hope you will enjoy it and the entire January 2017 *Quarterly Review* issue.

Sincerely,
Jacklyn DeMar, Esq.

Research & Grant Fraud: An Evolving Trend in False Claims Act Litigation

by Laura K. Wilk

Research and Grant Fraud:
An Evolving Trend in False Claims Act Litigation

Most practitioners and commentators in the False Claims Act arena are familiar with the rampant government procurement fraud that motivated Congress to conduct hearings between 1979 and 1986 and ultimately transform the False Claims Act ("FCA")[2] into the powerful fraud-fighting tool that it is today.[3] However, Congress's simultaneous interest in reducing scientific and research fraud has received much less attention. Compelled by separate media reports detailing four cases of research fabrication,[4] Congress also began conducting parallel hearings between 1981 and 1988 in an attempt to revamp research agency misconduct and anti-fraud policies in order to prevent future scientific fraud.[5] This convergence of congressional interests in strengthening the FCA and deterring research fraud sheds light onto a perplexity within FCA litigation: despite the clear congressional interest in unearthing and combating scientific and research fraud, only a scant number of FCA cases have been filed alleging research falsification. In fact, the first research falsification *qui tam* suit alleging scientific misconduct against an institution was not brought until 1995,[6] nearly a decade after Congress addressed the rise of research falsification and enacted the 1986 FCA amendments. This disparity raises questions over why, despite congressional concern, research falsification receives such little attention from *qui tam* relators.

One possible explanation for this disparity is the nature of research falsification fraud itself. Given that falsification of research most often occurs in a university setting and under a government grant, it creates unique—and often fatal—pitfalls that might dissuade potential research fraud relators. These pitfalls span both substantive and non-substantive issues and have created a poor track record for research falsification

---

1. J.D. Candidate, University of Texas School of Law. Edited by Jacklyn DeMar and Robert Patten

2. False Claims Amendments Act of 1986, Pub. L. No. 99-562, 100 Stat. 3153, codified as amended at 31 U.S.C.A. §§ 3729 to 3733 (1994)

3. See *False Claims Act of 1979, S. 1981: Hearing before the Subcommittee on Improvements in Judicial Machinery of the Committee on the Judiciary,* 96th Cong. (1979); See *False Claims Reform Act: Hearing before the Subcommittee on Administrative Practice and Procedure of the Committee on the Judiciary,* 99th Cong. (1985); See *Defense Procurement Fraud Law Enforcement: Hearing before the Subcommittee on Administrative Practice and Procedure of the Committee on the Judiciary,* 99th Cong. (1985).; See *False Claims Act Amendments: Hearing before the Subcommittee on Administrative Law and Governmental Relations of the Committee on the Judiciary* 99th Cong. (1986); See *Overview of False Claims and Fraud Legislation: Hearing before the Committee on the Judiciary,* 99th Cong. (1986).; James B. Helmer Jr., *False Claims Act: Incentivizing Integrity for 150 Years for Rogues, Privateers, Parasites and Patriots,* 81 U. Cin. L. Rev. 4 (2013) at 1271.

4. Barry D. Gold, Responsible Science: Ensuring the Integrity of the Research Process: Volume II 117-125 (National Academy of Sciences, 1993).

5. See *Fraud in Biomedical Research: Hearing before the Committee on Science and Technology, Subcommittee on Investigations and Oversight,* 97th Cong. (1981).; *Research Publication and Practices: Hearing before the Committee on Science and Technology, Task Force on Science Policy,* 99th Cong. (1986).; *Scientific Fraud and Misconduct and the Federal Response: Hearing before the Committee on Government Operations, Subcommittee on Human Resources and Intergovernmental Relations,* 100th Cong. (1988); *Scientific Fraud: Hearings Before the Subcommittee on Oversight and Investigations of the House Committee on Energy and Commerce,* 101st Cong. (1989); *Fraud in NIH Grant Programs: Hearing before the Committee on Energy and Commerce, Subcommittee on Oversight and Investigations,* 100th Cong. (1989).; *Maintaining the Integrity of Scientific Research: Hearing before the Committee on Energy and Commerce, Subcommittee on Oversight and Investigations,* 101st Cong. (1990).

6. Susan E. Sherman, *The False Claims Act: Litigating Scientific Misconduct,* 110 Pub. Health Works 784, 784 (1995).

Vol. 83 • January 2017   3

fraud cases.[7] A notable exception, however, is the case *United States ex rel. Krahling v. Merck & Company, Inc.*,[8] in which the relators survived a motion to dismiss their falsified research claims. This uncommon success serves as an exemplar for analyzing how to successfully allege a research falsification case given the numerous pitfalls that lie in the relator's path.

This article contrasts *Krahling's* successful survival of a motion to dismiss for failure to state a claim under Rule 12(b)(6) against its failed predecessors in order to assist counsel in understanding how to successfully plead falsified research fraud under the FCA. Accordingly, this analysis reveals that falsified research fraud pleadings are most likely to succeed when counsel alleges fraud under a theory of legal falsity based on a failure to meet a required duty to the relevant agency or government entity ("duty-based theory") as opposed to conventional theories of factual or legal falsity based on omissions ("omissions-based theory"). To demonstrate why duty-based theories frame cases most favorably, Part I will review *Krahling* itself, including the relator's allegations and the court's response. Part II will examine how *Krahling's* allegations differed from those of its predecessors and why the difference was consequential. Part III will note important differences that distinguish *Krahling* from its predecessors and, critically, why these distinctions do not diminish the effectiveness of a duty-based theory. Part IV will explore three non-substantive issues that plague relators bringing research fraud cases under the FCA, including the FCA's Statute of Limitations ("SOL"), Sovereign Immunity, and the Public Disclosure Bar.

PART I: *UNITED STATES EX REL. KRAHLING V. MERCK & COMPANY, INC.*

As this analysis will demonstrate, falsified research fraud cases are susceptible to numerous pitfalls that historically have proved fatal to most relators' claims. However, in *United States ex rel. Krahling v. Merck & Company, Inc.*, the United States District Court for the Middle District of North Carolina recently denied the defendant's motion to dismiss the relators' falsified research allegations for failure to state a claim under Rule 12(b)(6) and failure to plead fraud with particularity under Rule 9(b). What did the *Krahling* relators do differently to overcome these challenges? The answer to this question is the crux of Part II. However, before delving into *Krahling's* arguments, it is essential to understand the allegations of fraudulent conduct at the center of the case.

In *Krahling*, the relators alleged that their former employer, a pharmaceutical manufacturer and the United States' chief Measles Mumps and Rubella Vaccine ("MMR Vaccine") supplier, manipulated data in its clinical study in order to give the false impression that its vaccine was 95 percent effective.[9] The relators alleged that they witnessed the defendant knowingly alter a clinical study by manipulating blood samples and deviating from the "gold standard" of vaccine testing to fraudulently produce a

---

7. Excluding the pending cases *United States ex rel. Krahling v. Merck Co.*, 44 F.Supp.3d 581 (E.D. Pa. 2014) and *United States ex rel. Thomas v. Duke Univ.*, No. 1:17-cv-00276-CCE-JLW, (M.D.N.C. 2017), the only successful research falsification fraud cases were settled out of court.

8. 44 F. Supp. 3d 581 (E.D. Pa. 2014).

9. *Id.* at 588.

finding of increased vaccine efficacy.[10] The relators alleged FCA violations under two theories. First, the relators alleged that as a result of the vaccine's diminished efficacy, the vaccine label and package insert misrepresented the product that the government purchased from the defendant. Second, they alleged that the defendant violated multiple duties to relevant agencies and the government by failing to disclose "falsified, abandoned, and manipulated data" and its impact on the vaccine's efficacy.[11] The latter theory distinguishes *Krahling* from its predecessors.[12] Crucially, by focusing on whether the defendant fulfilled its duties to relevant agencies and the government, the *Krahling* relators framed their case so that the court would focus on the integrity of the financial relationship between the government and the defendant—a critical consideration that is often submerged under the theories asserted by *Krahling's* predecessors. In essence, *Krahling* stands out because its duty-based theory creates a framework that avoids many of the pitfalls that have befallen past falsified research relators.

PART II: *KRAHLING'S* FAVORABLE FRAMEWORK

A. The failings of a factual falsity theory

One particularly pernicious pitfall that *Krahling's* duty-based theory overcomes is the argument that the alleged research fraud is not fraud at all, but merely a scientific dispute or the result of a difference in scientific opinion, and thus not actionable under the FCA. In falsified research fraud cases, defendants typically raise the "scientific disagreement argument" when relators allege fraud on the basis of factual falsity. Such allegations generally take shape in a relator's argument that the defendant's statements to the government were false or inaccurate because they included fabricated or manipulated data as support for a grant application or progress report.[13] In response, the defendant often contends that the relator's allegations cannot sustain FCA liability because the statements were not "objectively false" or material to the grant award decision and amount only to "expressions of opinion . . . about which reasonable minds may differ." Such differences, defendants argue, should be resolved by the scientific community or relevant agency, not by the courts. [14]

   United States ex rel. Hill v. University of Medicine & Dentistry exemplifies this interchange, highlighting the difficulty in alleging falsity using a factual falsity theory

---

10. *Id.* at 587.

11. Amended Complaint with Jury Trial Demand at ¶ 2; *Krahling*, 44 F. Supp. 3d at 588.

12. *But see United States ex rel. Jones v. Brigham and Women's Hosp.*, 678 F.3d 72, 91-92 (1st Cir. 2012) (affirming the district court's decision to grant defendant's motion for summary judgment on the relator's allegations that the defendant failed to meet its duty to report falsified scientific results to NIH because the relator first raised the allegations in its opposition to the defendant's motion for summary judgment.) *Krahling* remains the first case to receive a favorable opinion using a duty-based theory. This article will revisit *Jones* in Part II.

13. *See generally United States ex rel. Prevenslik v. Univ. of Wa.*, No. A. MJG-02-80, 2013 WL 23573424 (D. Ma. 2003); *United States ex rel. Jones v. Brigham and Women's Hosp.*, 750 F. Supp.2d 358 (D. Mass. 2010); *United States ex rel. Hill v. Univ. of Med. & Dentistry of N.J.*, 448 Fed. Appx. 314 (3rd Cir. 2011); *United States ex rel. Milam v. Regents of University of California*, 912 F. Supp. 868 (D. Md. 1995).

14. *United States ex rel. Roby v. Boeing Co.*, 100 F. Supp. 2d 619, 625 (S.D. Ohio 2000).

in fraudulent research cases and demonstrating how *Krahling's* duty-based theory can prevail against these complications.[15] In *Hill*, the relator brought a *qui tam* action against the research lab where she was formerly employed, alleging that the defendant violated the FCA by knowingly using contaminated cell cultures in preliminary experiments to obtain results that would support its National Institute of Health ("NIH") grant application.[16] As a collaborative researcher engaged in the preliminary experiments, the relator raised concerns to the defendant that its data "failed to follow proper scientific protocol," but the defendant ignored her concerns and included statements detailing the allegedly fabricated results in its NIH grant application anyway.[17] The relator alleged that the data manipulation caused irreproducible results and constituted evidence of both falsity and scienter because the defendant's own intra-laboratory experiments failed to replicate the results. [18] The defendant raised the "scientific disagreement argument," emphasizing that the relator's concentration on the data's replicability highlighted that at its core, the relator's allegations were merely "scientific scrutiny," amounting to nothing more than "subjective analysis and disagreement" over experimental methods. [19] The United States District Court for the District of New Jersey granted the defendant's motion for summary judgment, and on appeal the United States Court of Appeals for the Third Circuit affirmed the district court's decision, holding that the "plaintiff presented evidence only demonstrating a scientific disagreement over the reliability of data," and thus could not establish falsity or scienter.[20] Despite their disparate outcomes, *Hill* and *Krahling* share many similarities in their fact patterns: both relators witnessed the contested research;[21] both reported concerns to internal and external authorities;[22] and the presiding agency did not discover fraudulent activity on its own.[23] Nevertheless, the courts applied different analyses and came to opposite conclusions, primarily because the *Krahling* court focused on the defendant's duty to the government as a recipient of funds rather than solely on the false statements it made in support of its claims.

By focusing on the defendant's duty, *Krahling* was able to circumvent the scientific disagreement argument that defeated the claims in *Hill* because it shifted the inquiry away from the question of whether the alleged manipulated data was false and toward the concept of duty. With this shift, the court was no longer limited to an examination of scientific results, accuracy, or methodology—a task arguably outside the court's expertise. Instead, the court was asked to analyze falsity by discerning if an express or implied legal duty existed—a task better suited for judicial resolution. This shift to a

---

15. 448 Fed. Appx. 314 (3rd Cir. 2011).

16. *Id.* at 315.

17. *Id.*

18. *Id.* at 317.

19. Motion for Summary Judgment at 16-17, *Hill*, 448 Fed. Appx. 314.

20. *Hill*, 448 Fed. Appx. at 317

21. *See id.* at 315; *Krahling*, 44 F. Supp. 3d at 587

22. *See Hill*, 448 Fed. Appx. at 315; *Krahling*, 44 F. Supp. 3d at 587.

23. *See Hill*, 448 Fed. Appx. at 316; *Krahling*, 44 F. Supp. 3d at 587.

duty-based theory creates a greater likelihood that a relator alleging falsified research will survive a motion to dismiss or for summary judgment and sidestep the topic of "science" altogether.

Courts often exercise caution in making determinations of a scientific nature. By turning the court's focus away from scientific inquiry and toward the legal concept of duty, the relator helps to undermine the common defense argument that plaintiffs seek to transform the FCA into an "all-purpose antifraud statue."[24] Research fraud is a niche area that draws a fine line between weighing in on how experiments and research ought to be done and ferreting out truly fraudulent actors in the research field. The objective of a meritorious falsified research fraud case is the latter, and it is critical to make that fact apparent when alleging research fraud. *Krahling's* duty-based theory does exactly that; it frames the case to center on what is important within the FCA context—the integrity of the financial relationship between the government and defendant—and sifts out the topically unimportant, *i.e.* research methodology and scientific variance.

This reasoning is illuminated in *United States ex rel. Milam v. The Regents of the University of California.*[25] Like *Hill*, the *Milam* relator employed a theory of factual falsity based upon the inclusion of manipulated research results in a grant application. Specifically, the relator alleged that the defendant knowingly and "irreconcilably deviated"[26] from commonly accepted scientific practices, consequently producing "non-data"[27] that it characterized as legitimate in its NIH grant application.[28] The United States District Court for the District of Maryland granted the defendant's motion for summary judgment, finding that the relator failed to state a claim.[29] In particular, the court found that the statements that the relator alleged were untrue were at most a "legitimate scientific dispute," explaining that the relator failed to demonstrate any support for the argument that the data did not actually comply with the scientific method.[30] As in *Hill*, the *Milam* relator failed to narrow the case to clearly address the relevant financial relationship, causing the court to view its role in the case as deciphering "good science" from "bad science." Had the relator employed a duty-based theory, s/he may well have avoided the scientific disagreement argument and improved her/his likelihood of success. The *Milam* court's analysis of the relator's theory of liability further underscores a factual falsity theory's susceptibility to fatal falsity arguments and common scienter pitfalls, and illuminates how *Krahling's* duty-based argument can help to circumvent these entanglements.

Another barrier faced by relators who allege research fraud under a factual falsity theory is the argument that even if the statements were false, the defendant could not

---

24. *Allison Engine Co., Inc. v. United States ex rel. Sanders*, 128 S. Ct. 2123, 2130 (2008).

25. 912 F. Supp. 868 (D. Md. 1995).

26. *Id.* at 886.

27. *Id.* at 878.

28. *Id.*

29. 912 F. Supp. at 891.

30. *Id.* at 886.

have possessed the requisite scienter because the false statements were merely a matter of negligence, mistake, or "scientific error."[31] This argument, like the scientific disagreement inquiry, is likely to create fatal ambiguity for relators alleging FCA liability based on fraudulent research. A court's analysis can become muddied because of the difficulty in discerning whether the contested actions were rooted in science or fraud, and the *Milam* decision provides a clear example of these difficulties.[32] The *Milam* court granted the defendant summary judgment on the issue of scienter, explaining that the relator had failed to provide evidence that the statements were knowingly false. Allowing a jury trial would, the court reasoned, be an "unconscionable intrusion of law on academia ... [because] scientists would be forced to report all varying results."[33] Under the factual falsity theory, the court raised the same concerns regarding both scienter and falsity, and found that the allegations fall within the realm of scientific skill or discretion and outside the scope of the court's authority.

A duty-based theory can avoid these traps by shifting the scienter discussion away from the research itself and instead to a discussion of whether the defendants knew of their alleged failure to meet a required duty,[34] but this shift in focus is not as clear-cut when considering scienter as it is when considering falsity. Relators must still allege that research defendants were aware that their conduct violated their duty to the government or that they acted with reckless disregard of that duty.[35] Nevertheless, a relator has a greater likelihood of surviving a motion to dismiss or for summary judgment if it creates a foothold for scienter analysis in a context outside of science.

United States ex rel. Jones v. Brigham and Women's Hospital[36] is *Krahling's* only predecessor to survive the pleading stage under a factual falsity theory, and it demonstrates how even a minor shift in context away from scientific inquiry critically alters the outcome in a falsified research case. Though the relator in *Brigham and Women's Hospital* ultimately failed to prevail at trial, he was able to survive the defendant's motion for summary judgment. He had alleged that the defendants deviated from the scientific protocol that they reported in their NIH grant application and instead cherry-picked and manipulated data so that they could produce statistically significant results.[37] The United States Court of Appeals for the First Circuit reversed the district court's grant of summary judgment for the defendant, explaining in detail why the

---

31. *Wang v. FMC Corp.*, 975 F.2d 1412, 1421 (9th Cir. 1992).

32. *Milam* also demonstrates a less prevalent scienter issue in the falsified research arena, specifically, that the hierarchical structure of labs can lead to trouble alleging scienter unless a relator can allege knowledge on the part of the person who signed the grant application. This duty is often delegated to a lower level employee that may not have knowledge of the fraud. *See Milam*, 912 F. Supp. at 887-88 (explaining that the director signing grant applications did not possess requisite scienter because he was not a researcher, and thus "was entitled to delegate responsibility for scientific accuracy to his subordinates").

33. *Milam*, 912 F. Supp. at 889.

34. *Krahling*, 44 F. Supp. 3d at 595 (explaining that the relators alleged scienter through first-hand accounts of the defendant violating its duties to report diminished efficacy).

35. 31 U.S.C. § 3729 (2017)(b)(1).

36. 678 F.3d 72 (1st Cir. 2014)

37. *Id.* at 77-79.

relator's false statements constituted more than a mere "scientific judgment."[38] The circuit court noted that "all the measurements in question were purportedly generated by a single protocol that [the defendants] agreed to before beginning."[39] Thus, it appears the relator succeeded where other allegations of factual falsity failed because he was able to direct the court to a very specific set of norms and protocols that were agreed to in the bargain with the government. Furthermore, the relator alleged that one researcher was responsible for all cherry-picking,[40] allowing him to pinpoint exactly where the manipulation occurred and how it affected the outcome of the research.[41]

The relator in *Brigham and Women's Hospital* alleged favorable facts for a research fraud case, but it was not the facts alone that permitted him to survive summary judgment, but also the legal framework that the facts were able to generate. The circuit court noted that:

> The dispute at the heart of this case is not about resolving which scientific protocol produces results that fall within the acceptable range of "accuracy." Nor is it about whether [the defendant's] re-measurements . . . are "accurate" insofar as they fall within a range of results accepted by qualified experts. Rather, *the essential dispute is about whether [the defendant] falsified scientific data by intentionally exaggerating the [results] to cause proof of a particular scientific hypothesis to emerge from the data* [emphasis added].[42]

The court scrutinizes the defendant's actions, mirroring the focus in *Krahling* on a duty-based theory of liability. The opinion states explicitly that the case centers on the defendant's conduct, not the result of its research, and concentrates on the integrity of the grant, not the resolution of scientific quibbles.

The relator in *Brigham and Women's Hospital* was able to create this framework through allegations of factual falsity in the defendant's research methodology, but many research fraud relators are not so fortunate. As both *Krahling* and *Brigham and Women's Hospital* demonstrate, a duty-based theory may increase a relator's chances of creating this framework in a falsified research case by effectively guiding the court to focus primarily on the actions of the defendants and their financial relationship with the government, and not on the science itself. This shift in focus will also prove helpful to relators who use a theory of legal falsity to bring falsified research claims on based upon the omission of material facts.

---

38. *Id.* at 88 ("the revision in question does not implicate questions of scientific judgment as the district court suggested").

39. *Id.*

40. *Id.* at 77.

41. *Id.* at 81.

42. *Id.* at 96.

B. Failings of an omissions-based theory

As with a factual falsity theory, the allegations supporting a relator's omission-based theory typically focus solely on the statements contained in the grant application or progress reports. Ordinarily, the relator alleges that the defendant intentionally omitted information that was material to the relevant agency's grant award and, by choosing to exclude the omitted information, presented a false application and misled the agency.[43] Relators who have employed this theory consistently confront the argument that they failed to demonstrate that the omissions were material to the government's grant award decision, and thus failed to allege an FCA violation.[44] Krahling's duty-based theory sidesteps this argument by means of the relator's identification of a statutory, regulatory, or contractual obligation that the defendant failed to meet.[45] By pointing to an expressly stated government expectation, the relator guides the court away from the question of whether the falsified data was material, and instead to an inquiry into whether the defendant's breach of its duty was material to the government's payment decision. The relator's complaint remains vulnerable to the argument that there was no duty, or that the alleged violation was not material, but guiding the court away from scientific inquiry puts the relator in a better position to successfully oppose dispositive motions.

Milam demonstrates how an omissions-based theory commonly proceeds, and why a duty-based approach is more effective. The relator in Milam employed an omissions-based theory of liability and alleged that the defendants failed to disclose in their NIH grant application that previously cited data was inaccurate and that one researcher's data was false,[46] and the United States District Court for the District of Maryland granted the defendant's motion for summary judgment.[47] The court addressed each omission separately, first explaining that the relator failed to offer a "reason why the omission of previously cited data would be a false statement,"[48] particularly because the FCA "does not impose liability unless the defendant has an obligation to disclose the omitted information."[49] Next, the court explained that the relator did not provide sufficient evidence that the defendant possessed a "statutory, regulatory, or fiduciary obligation" to disclose the false data.[50] The Milam relator's complaint would have been stronger if she had linked her allegations to an express requirement or duty.

---

43. See generally Milam, 912 F. Supp. 868; United States ex rel. Berge v. The Board of Trustees of the Univ. of Ala., 104 F.3d 1453 (4th Cir. 1996); United States ex rel. Bauchwitz, M.D. v. Holloman, 671 F. Supp.2d 674 (E.D. Pa. 2009).

44. See generally Milam, 912 F .Supp. 868; Berge, 104 F.3d 145.

45. Krahling, 44 F. Supp. 3d at 594-95.

46. Milam, 912 F. Supp. at 884.

47. Id. at 885.

48. This case was decided prior to the Supreme Court's decision in Universal Health Serv., Inc. v. United States ex rel. Escobar, 136 S.Ct. 1989 (2016). The district court's analysis may change after consideration of the Supreme Court's holding that if a defendant omits pertinent information from the representations included in a submission "liability may attach if the omission renders those representations misleading." Id. at 1995.

49. Milam, 912 F. Supp. at 884.

50. Id.

Employing *Krahling's* duty-based theory would have helped overcome these vulner-abilities because it requires identification of an express duty and focuses the case on the financial relationship between the defendant and the government rather than the materiality or falsity of the actual research.

While *Milam* serves as a primer for why omissions-based allegations often fail, the court did not explore the materiality issues that arise under omission-based al-legations. The decision in *United States ex rel. Berge v. The Board of Trustees of the University of Alabama* elucidates these materiality issues.[51] The relator in *Berge* used an omissions-based theory to allege that the defendants submitted NIH grant appli-cations containing misleading conclusions about their research. The relator brought a *qui tam* suit against the university where she earned her Ph.D. and against indi-vidual researchers and professors,[52] alleging that the defendants misled NIH when they failed to include the relator's involvement and findings in their progress reports.[53] She alleged that her findings were material to NIH's continued grant award because they refuted the defendants' previously published data and central hypothesis.[54] The United States District Court for the District of Maryland awarded the relator nearly $2 million after she prevailed at trial,[55] but the United States Court of Appeals for the Fourth Circuit reversed the decision, holding that the district court erred in denying the defendants' motion for judgment as a matter of law. The circuit court found that the relator failed to meet "her burden of showing materiality."[56] The court explained that it was "hard to imagine that NIH's decision-making could have been influenced by [the omission that the relator alleged]" because the grant award could not possibly depend on the relator's work or the inclusion of her name.[57] It appears evident that the court rejected relator's omissions-based theory because it did not find an express ex-pectation or requirement that would permit it to determine that the alleged omissions were material. The circuit court in *Berge* cites *Milam* for the proposition that liability exists only where the defendant "has an obligation to disclose omitted information."[58] The decisions in *Berge* and *Milam* strongly suggest that, although the differences be-tween omissions-based and duty-based theories are nuanced, a relator asserting the latter has a better chance of success because she has founded her allegations on an identifiable legal duty.

---

51. 104 F.3d 1453 (4th Cir. 1997)

52. *Id.* at 1455.

53. *Id.* at 1456.

54. Amended Complaint at ¶51-55, *Berge*, 104 F.3d. 1453 (D. Md. 1997).

55. Susan E. Sherman, *The False Claims Act: Litigating Scientific Misconduct*, 110 Pub. Health Works 784, 784 (1995).

56. *Berge*, 104 F.3d. at 1462.

57. *Id.*

58. *Id.* at 1461.

PART III: APPLICATION OF *KRAHLING* IN THE GRANT CONTEXT

Krahling involves a government purchasing decision, rather than a grant award, and there is a striking distinction between the case and its predecessors. This distinction is particularly evident when considering the wrongdoing that the relator alleged: failure to meet regulatory, statutory, and contractual duties requiring "accurate and up-to-date information" on the safety and effectiveness of vaccines,[59] and the duty to "be forthcoming and honest with federal officials in all of its dealings with the government."[60] At first blush, this difference seems weighty as a matter of science, considering that many of the duties identified *Krahling* related to the development and production of vaccines: a regulated *object*, not grant-based research. However, this distinction does not diminish the strength of *Krahling's* duty-based theory, and a pending case brought after *Krahling* was filed, *United States ex rel. Thomas v. Duke University*,[61] has also succeeded in alleging falsified research fraud in the context of an NIH grant award using a duty-based theory.

In *Duke University*, the relator alleged that, for over a decade, the defendant systematically produced and published falsified or "simply made up" data in reports to the government in order to obtain research grants from NIH, the Environmental Protection Agency ("EPA"), and other federal agencies.[62] The relator applied *Krahling's* duty-based theory to grant fraud by alleging that the defendant "failed to comply with its affirmative duty to protect grant funds from misuse, failed to ensure the integrity of work supported by grant funds, . . . failed to foster a research environment that discourages research misconduct, and failed to deal forthrightly with possible research misconduct as required by the Regulations."[63] These allegations apply a duty-based theory in the grant context as *Krahling* utilized it in a purchasing context. Like the plaintiff in *Krahling*, the *Duke University* relator alleged that the defendants created false data and omitted critical information, and argued that FCA liability arose from the defendant's failure to comply with duties inherent in the grant application process, not from the false data or omissions themselves. The United States District Court for the Middle District of North Carolina denied the defendant's motion to dismiss for failure to state a claim under Rule 12(b)(6), moving the case forward to discovery.[64] While the court did not issue an opinion on its order, the arguments that the defendants presented against the relator demonstrate that *Krahling's* duty-based strategy does not hinge on a government purchasing decision, but can also effectively frame a grant fraud case.

Though the *Duke University* relator brought a *qui tam* suit against individual researchers and the University itself, he applied the duty-based theory only against the

---

59. Amended Complaint with Jury Trial Demand at ¶ 103-114, *Krahling*, 44 F. Supp. 3d 581.

60. *Id.* at ¶ 120.

61. No. 1:17-cv-00276-CCE-JLW (M.D.N.C. 2017).

62. Amended Complaint at ¶ 3-4, *Duke Univ.*, No. 15-4374 (W.D. Va. April 25, 2017).

63. *Id.* at ¶ 224.

64. *Duke Univ.*, No. 1:17-cv-00276-CCE-JLW (M.D.N.C. April, 25 2017).

university.[65] The defendant university's memorandum in support of its motion to dismiss centered largely on the question of whether the defendants submitted "any actual, false claim[s]" for payment and whether the alleged duties were material to the government's payment decision under *Universal Health Services v. United States ex rel. Escobar*.[66] The relator was able to overcome these arguments and frame his allegations as *Krahling* did in the purchasing context, consequently guiding the court to focus on the financial relationship and the violation of the duties rather than on the underlying science. Nevertheless, the relator did not entirely avoid the "scientific disagreement" argument, as the university defendants briefly argued in their memorandum that liability could not attach to "scientific judgments," citing *Hill*.[67] However, the defendants spent far less time on this argument than they did on the issue of whether actual claims were submitted and whether the regulatory duties were material under *Escobar*.[68] This disparity is striking when considering that past defendants have focused most heavily on the scientific disagreement objection, and further demonstrates that the duty-based theory effectively shifts the dispositive issues within the case to increase the likelihood of a favorable outcome for the relator. [69] Overall, *Duke University* clarifies that *Krahling's* duty-based theory is as effective in a grant decision case as it was for the *Krahling* relator in a government purchasing decision. In both cases the relators relied on a duty-based theory to survive motions to dismiss and evade the common and usually fatal vulnerabilities of their predecessors.

PART IV: NON-SUBSTANTIVE ISSUES PREVALENT IN FALSIFIED RESEARCH FRAUD CASES

Although employing a duty-based theory of liability is useful in framing these cases, relators' counsel must also be conscious of several non-substantive issues prevalent in the research fraud arena. Some of these pitfalls include the FCA's Statute of Limitations ("SOL"), sovereign immunity preclusions, and the public disclosure bar. These non-substantive issues arise primarily due to the nature of academia and scientific research, where nearly all falsified research fraud cases arise. With a grasp of these issues and concerns, relators and their attorneys can approach a falsified research case with a better understanding of the road ahead and an increased chance of success.

A. Statute of Limitations

Most falsified data frauds occur under government grants, many of them in the context of an NIH grant. For example, in fiscal year 2016 NIH's budget comprised just

---

65. Amended Complaint at ¶ 3-4, *Duke Univ.*, No. 15-4374 (W.D. Va. April 25, 2017).

66. Brief/Memorandum in Support at 1, *Duke Univ.*, No. 15-4374; *Universal Health Services v. U.S. ex rel. Escobar*, 579 U.S. —, 136 S. Ct. 1989 (2016).

67. Brief/Memorandum in Support at 17, *Duke Univ.*, No. 15-4374.

68. *Id.*

69. *Compare, e.g. id. with* Brief in Support of Motion for Summary Judgment at 6-17, *Hill* 448 Fed.Appx. 314.

over half of the total federal science research budget.[70] However, NIH's grant process often leads to SOL barriers for falsified research relators. In short, NIH awards grants on a competitive basis and typically approves grants in their entirety.[71] NIH then releases the grant incrementally on an annual basis, requiring the grant recipient to submit progress reports to NIH detailing the recipient's research progress in the previous year in order to justify the continued release of funds.[72] Critically, the progress reports require significantly less information about the recipient's research than the initial grant application, and only require recipients to certify the truth and accuracy of the information included in the progress report.[73] Due to this framework, courts generally hold that the SOL begins running at the time of the initial grant application[74] because that is when the recipient fraudulently induced the government to award the grant.[75] These parameters often result in the dismissal of research fraud cases because defendants used falsified data only in their initial grant application to induce a grant award, but submitted technically truthful progress reports.[76] While these reports are considered claims for payment,[77] they are often substantially less detailed and only certify the truth of the information they contain, and therefore do not include the essential false information that gave rise to the fraud. As a result, if the original grant application was submitted outside of the SOL term, courts often hold that the relator's case cannot survive. Importantly, the Supreme Court's decision in Escobar, which recognized the implied false certification theory of liability, might remove some SOL barriers for falsified research relators, who can argue that the progress reports impliedly certify the truthfulness of the information contained in the initial grant application.[78]

The decision in *United States ex rel. Bauchwitz v. Holloman* helps unpack the SOL issue.[79] In *Bauchwitz*, the relator alleged that the defendants intentionally used publications and research findings that were based on false research as the basis of their initial NIH grant application, yet certified the accuracy of their subsequent progress reports without correcting the initial misrepresentations.[80] The United States District Court for the Eastern District of Pennsylvania granted the defendants' motion for

---

70. Jeffrey Mervis, *Updated: Budget agreement boosts U.S. science*, Science (Dec. 18, 2015), http://www.sciencemag.org/news/2015/12/updated-budget-agreement-boosts-us-science#table.

71. Nat'l. Inst. of Health, *Pre-Award and Award Process*, https://grants.nih.gov/grants/pre-award-process.htm. (last visited June 28, 2017).

72. Nat'l. Inst. of Health, *Post-Award Monitoring and Reporting*, https://grants.nih.gov/grants/post-award-monitoring-and-reporting.htm. (last visited June 28, 2017).

73. *Bauchwitz*, 671 F. Supp.2d at 680.

74. *But see* 31 U.S.C. § 3731(b)(2) (2017).

75. *Bauchwitz*, 671 F. Supp. 2d at 688 (explaining that the nature of the grant process requires NIH to award grants at the exclusion of other research projects). Thus, if relying on a false application, NIH suffers at the time the application is made, not at the release of payment, because the initial award decision caused NIH to lose the research benefits that it otherwise would have gained.

76. *See, e.g. Bauchwitz*, 671 F. Supp. 2d 674.

77. *Id.* at 688-690.

78. *Escobar*, 579 U.S.—, 136 S. Ct. 1989.

79. *Bauchwitz*, 671 F. Supp. 2d 674.

80. *Id.* at 679.

summary judgment on all but one of the relator's claims, finding that the claims were time-barred.[81] The court explained that the certification of accuracy in the progress report "is limited to the truth and accuracy of the progress reports themselves," and therefore the relator could not connect the progress reports to the initial grant application.[82] The court found that the relator relied on an implied false certification theory of liability not recognized in the Third Circuit, so the relator's allegations could not give rise to liability.[83] That analysis would likely differ in the wake of *Escobar*, but the court noted that the relator's allegations would have failed regardless because he did not identify a specific regulation that the defendants violated.[84]

Falsified research relators commonly base their allegations on the relationship between progress reports and the initial grant application, and *Bauchwitz* exemplifies why these cases have frequently encountered problems with the FCA's SOL. However, the Supreme Court's recognition of the implied false certification theory in *Escobar* may influence the way courts view this relationship, and may eliminate SOL barriers that prevented past relators from filing or succeeding in falsified research cases.

B. Sovereign Immunity

After the Supreme Court issued its decision in *Vermont Agency of Natural Resources v. United States ex rel. Stevens*, protection from FCA liability under the Eleventh Amendment became another prevalent non-substantive blockade in the research fraud arena.[85] Falsified research cases are particularly susceptible to this jurisdictional bar because most alleged frauds take place in academic research institutions, and many potential defendants are public colleges and universities. Under *Stevens*, state institutions are exempt from FCA liability because they qualify as "arms of the state." In fiscal year 2016, NIH—the agency with the largest science research budget[86]—allocated 80% of its research grant funding to higher education institutions. Of that funding, 60% was awarded to universities or colleges considered public institutions.[87] Given the significant amount of funding awarded to public institutions, it is unsurprising that many research fraud claims are jurisdictionally barred by sovereign immunity.

United States ex rel. King v. University of Texas Health Science Ctr. illustrates how a case will fail if a defendant qualifies as an arm of the state.[88] The King relator alleged that the defendant violated the FCA by falsifying research data to obtain federal

---

81. *Id.* at 705.

82. *Id.* at 690.

83. *Id.* at 690.

84. *Id.* at 691.

85. 529 U.S. 765 (2000).

86. *Supra* note 66.

87. U.S. Dept. of Health & Human Servs., *NIH Research Portfolio Online Reporting Tools (report): NIH Awards by Location & Organization*, https://www.report.nih.gov/award/index.cfm?ot=DH,27,47,4,52,64,10000,MS,20,16,6,13,10,49,53,86,OTHDH&fy=2017&state=&ic=&fm=&orgid=&distr=&rfa=&om=n&pid= (last visited June 29, 2017).

88. 544 Fed. Appx. 490 (5th Cir. 2013).

funding and by failing to obtain proper consent from human research subjects.[89] The United States District Court for the Southern District of Texas dismissed the relator's claims for failure to state a claim under Rule 12(b)(6), finding that the defendant was not a "person"[90] under the FCA, but rather a state entity exempt from FCA liability.[91] On appeal, the United States Court of Appeals for the Fifth Circuit affirmed the district court's decision.[92] Both the district and appellate court evaluated *King* under the arm-of-the-state six factor test delineated in *Clark v. Tarrant County, Texas*,[93] and concluded that the defendant was a state agency.[94] The circuit court explained that the defendant met five out of the six *Clark* factors, and importantly met the "most significant" factor: that a judgment against the defendant would be paid out of the state treasury, and thus would "interfere with the fiscal autonomy and political sovereignty of [the state]."[95] In practice, each institution's funding structure and relationship with the state will differ, and merely identifying a defendant as a public university is not dispositive of its entitlement to sovereign immunity protections. Nevertheless, the prevalence of grants and research awards to state universities will no doubt bar many falsified research cases.

C.   Public Disclosure Bar

The public disclosure bar[96] often creates a barrier to falsified research cases because the overarching goal in most scientific research is to produce publishable findings. Therefore, researchers rush to publish their findings or news outlets quickly report the researchers' results and studies, causing the information underlying many relators' allegations to become publicly disclosed.[97] Additionally, because the research is funded through government grants, the grant applications and other related material that might serve as the basis of relators' complaints could also be publicly disclosed.[98] Some relators are able to overcome the public disclosure bar through the "original source" exception because they themselves were engaged in the research at the center of the suit. Others, however, will encounter public disclosure arguments.

In *United States ex rel. Lewis v. Walker*,[99] for instance, the EPA awarded a grant to the defendants to conduct technical research on sewage sludge toxicity in a single

---

89. *Id.* at 492.

90. 31 U.S.C. § 3729(a)(1) (2017).

91. *United States ex rel. King v. Univ. of Tex. Health Science Ctr.*, 907 F. Supp. 2d 846 (S.D. Tex. 2012).

92. *King*, 544 Fed. Appx. at 499.

93. 798 F.2d 736 (5th Cir. 1986).

94. *Compare with King*, 907 F. Supp.2d at 846.

95. *King*, 544 Fed. Appx. at 496.

96. 31 U.S.C. § 3730(4).

97. See, *e.g., United States ex rel. Prevenslik v. The Univ. of Wash.*, No. Civ. A. MJG-02-80, 2003 WL 23573424 at *3 (D. Md. 2003).

98. See, *e.g., Berge*, 104 F.3d at 1453 (explaining that the relator obtained the defendant's grant applications through Freedom of Information Act ["FOIA"] requests).

99. 438 Fed. Appx. 885 (11th Cir. 2011).

municipality in order to evaluate whether the sewage sludge caused significant cattle death and damage to dairy farms.[100] Through separate litigation related to the cattle deaths and dairy farm damage, the relators alleged that they became aware that the defendants fraudulently obtained the EPA grant by submitting false statements about their data collection methods and including published conclusions based on falsified data.[101] The relators brought the *qui tam* suit alleging that the defendants submitted false statements to the government, using the grant application and correspondence between defendants that they obtained through a FOIA request as their primary support.[102] The United States District Court for the Middle District of Georgia's granted the defendants' motion to dismiss the relators' claims under the public disclosure bar, and the United States Court of Appeals for the Eleventh Circuit affirmed.[103] The circuit court explained that the relators' claims were barred because they relied on publicly disclosed administrative reports procured through a FOIA request and the relators could not demonstrate that they possessed "direct and independent knowledge"[104] to meet the original source exception because none of the relators were involved in the relevant research or grant application process.[105] By contrast, the relator in *Berge* obtained copies of the defendant's grant application through FOIA requests in order to bring suit, yet objections to the court's subject matter jurisdiction were not raised,[106] presumably because the relator was a collaborating researcher and thus qualified as an original source.[107] Because the information underlying falsified research allegations are frequently published by the researchers themselves, by the government, or by news outlets, a relator who is able to qualify as an original source of the information, either as a researcher or as a participant in the grant application process, will be much better positioned to survive a motion to dismiss on public disclosure grounds.

V. CONCLUSION

Reliance on a duty-based theory of liability increases a relator's likelihood of surviving a motion to dismiss or motion for summary judgment in a research and grant fraud case. The increased likelihood of success is grounded in the way a duty-based theory guides the court and frames the relator's allegations. A duty-based theory moves the court away from analyzing the actual research and instead to analyzing whether the defendant maintained its research responsibilities and the integrity of its financial relationship with the government. Relators who bring conventional falsified research

---

100. *United States ex rel. Lewis v. Walker*, 738 F. Supp.2d 1284, 1288 (M.D. Ga. 2010).

101. *Id.*

102. *Lewis*, 438 Fed. Appx. at 888.

103. *Id.*

104. P.L. 99-562, 100 Stat. 3153 (1986).

105. *Lewis*, 438 Fed. Appx. at 886-887.

106. *Berge*, 104 F.3d 1453 (4th Cir. 1997).

107. Note that within the falsified research arena, thus far only relators that were not involved in the relevant research or grant application have been precluded under the public disclosure bar.

fraud cases based upon factual falsity or an omissions-based theory will find that courts are reluctant to make judgments on how science ought to be performed. A falsified research case should not be centrally focused on the relevant science; rather, it should focus on the materiality of truthfulness in a government grant application and award, and the impropriety of conduct that is likely to result in wasted research funds and time. Falsified research cases should focus their allegations on what is most important, i.e. financial relationships and responsibilities to the government. The use of a duty-based theory increases the chances of a relator's success by avoiding fatal pitfalls, but also addresses and emphasizes why falsified research fraud is damaging to the public fisc and should be rooted out. Relators must also be conscious of non-substantive issues, such as the FCA's SOL, sovereign immunity, and public disclosure bars because these defenses are common in falsified research fraud cases. Understanding the prevalence of these non-substantive issues and relying upon a duty-based theory will improve a relator's chances of success in ferreting out research fraud and securing the recovery of taxpayer funds in an FCA action.

Recent False Claims Act & *Qui Tam* Decisions

OCTOBER 1, 2016–DECEMBER 31, 2016

FALSE CLAIMS ACT LIABILITY

A. Violations of the Anti-Kickback Statute and/or Stark Law

U.S. ex rel. Greenfield v. Medco Health Sys., Inc., 2016 WL 7408843 (D.N.J. Dec. 22, 2016)

Holding: The U.S. District Court for the District of New Jersey granted the defendants' motion for summary judgment on the relator's kickback allegations.

The relator brought a *qui tam* suit against the health services provider where he was formerly employed and its affiliates, alleging that the defendants violated the False Claims Act by falsely certifying compliance with the Anti-Kickback Statute and caused tainted claims to be submitted to the government. The relator alleged that the defendant engaged in a kickback scheme in which it made charitable contributions to a tax-exempt organization that works with hemophilia patients in order to "buy, influence, and induce" referrals for the defendants' hemophilia products. The defendants and the relator both moved for summary judgment.

The court granted the defendants' motion for summary judgment, concluding that the relator failed to demonstrate that the government would not have reimbursed the defendant if it had known about the alleged violations of the AKS. The court also held that the relator failed to demonstrate that any one of the defendants' hemophilia clients was linked to the defendants' charitable donations. Further, the court noted that the tax-exempt organization's policy of listing donors as "preferred providers" on its website did not create a causal connection between the defendants' donations and referrals.

U.S. ex rel. Ruscher v. Omnicare, Inc., 2016 WL 6407128 (5th Cir. Oct. 28, 2016)

Holding: The U.S. Court of Appeals for the Fifth Circuit affirmed the district court's decision to grant summary judgment to the defendant on relator's allegations stemming from Anti-Kickback Statue violations.

The relator brought a *qui tam* suit against the pharmacy services provider where she was formerly employed and its affiliates, alleging that the defendants violated the Anti-Kickback Statute ("AKS") by paying kickbacks in the form of non-collection of Medicare Part A debt and offering prompt payment discounts ("PPDs") to skilled nursing facilities ("SNFs") in exchange for patient referrals, and caused claims tainted by those kickbacks to be submitted to the government in violation of the False Claims Act. The relator also alleged that the defendant caused SNFs submit false cost reports, as the defendant did not pay for the reported costs within the required time. Further, during the time period that the realtor alleged, the defendants were obligated to report any potential fraud to the government pursuant to a Corporate Integrity Agreement ("CIA"). The relator alleged that the defendants violated the reverse false claims provision of the FCA by failing to report the fraud after she had informed her supervisors of her concerns via email. The U.S. District Court for the Southern District of Texas granted the defendants' motion for summary judgment and the relator appealed to the Fifth Circuit.

The circuit court affirmed the district court's decision to grant the defendant summary judgment. The court explained that the relator provided no evidence demonstrating that the SNFs knew how the defendant designed its negotiation settlements and debt collection practices or that the SNFs were aware of the benefits that they were receiving, which the court reasoned was necessary to prove the relator's alleged AKS violation. Furthermore, the court explained that the relator failed to show that defendant's PPDs were designed to induce referrals or offered illegitimately. The court also determined that the relator did not sufficiently allege that the defendant caused an SNF to submit a false cost report because the relator's evidence did not include the entire time period in which the defendant could have submitted costs. Finally, the circuit court affirmed the district court's summary judgment ruling on the relator's reverse false claims allegation, finding that the email that she wrote to her supervisors did not indicate a probable violation of federal health care laws such that it was reportable to the government under the CIA.

U.S. ex rel. Bingham v. HCA, Inc., 2016 WL 6027115 (S.D. Fla. Oct. 14, 2016)

> **Holding: The U.S. District Court for the Southern District of Florida granted the defendant's motion to dismiss for failure to plead fraud with particularity under Rule 9(b) on this Anti-Kickback Statute and Stark Law claims.**

The relator, a commercial real estate appraiser, brought a *qui tam* suit against his former employer's client, a national health care services provider, alleging that it violated the Stark Law and Anti-Kickback Statute through a fraudulent real estate scheme that illegally paid remuneration to referring physicians in the form of free parking benefits and equity interest. The relator alleged that the defendant violated the False Claims Act by submitting claims to the government tainted by these AKS and Stark Law violations. The defendant moved to dismiss the relator's claims for failure to plead with particularity pursuant to Rule 9(b), arguing that the relator impermissibly relied on information obtained through discovery to draft his Second Amended Complaint in order meet the particularity requirements of Rule 9(b).

The court granted the defendant's motion to dismiss, agreeing with the defendant that the relator could not plead the "who, what, where, when, and how" of his alleged fraud without information acquired in discovery, and his conclusory allegations were not sufficient to meet the requirements of Rule 9(b).

See *U.S. ex rel. Brown v. Celgene Corp.*, 2016 WL 7626222 (C.D. Cal. Dec. 28, 2016) at page 38.

See *State of New York ex rel. Khurana v. Spherion Corp.*, 2016 WL 6652735 (S.D.N.Y. Nov. 10, 2016) at page 41.

B. Procurement Fraud

U.S. ex rel. Berg v. Honeywell Int'l., Inc., 2016 WL 7478959 (D. Alaska Dec. 29, 2016)

> **Holding:** The U.S. District Court for the District of Alaska granted the defendants' motion for summary judgment on the relators' fraudulent-inducement claims, finding that the relators failed to present sufficient evidence that the defendant knowingly violated the False Claims Act.

The relators brought a *qui tam* suit against a government contractor and its subsidiaries alleging that they fraudulently induced the government into awarding them a contract to provide energy-saving improvements to Army buildings. The relators alleged that the defendants knowingly presented false calculations of sales, costs, and savings to the government in order to receive certain contracts in violation of the False Claims Act. The defendants moved for summary judgment, arguing that they made extensive disclosures to the government about the underlying calculations and data in an open and collaborative process, thus they could not have the requisite scienter to defraud the government in violation of the FCA.

The court granted the defendants' motion for summary judgment. The court concluded that the defendants could not be liable under the FCA for misrepresenting projected sales because the defendants disclosed extensive, transparent calculations to the government, and the relator failed to demonstrate that the defendant knew its projected savings costs were inaccurate. Additionally, the court found that the relators did not provide any evidence to demonstrate that the defendants did not use due diligence in reaching their projected numbers.

U.S. ex rel. Keaveney v. SRA Int'l, Inc., 2016 WL 6988787 (D.D.C. Nov. 29, 2016)

> **Holding:** The U.S. District Court for the District of Columbia granted the defendants' motion to dismiss the relator's allegations that the defendants submitted false claims pursuant to their government contract for failure to state a claim under Rule 12(b)(6) and failure to plead fraud with particularity under Rule 9(b) in part.

The relator brought a *qui tam* suit against a government defense contractor, Systems Research and Applications Corporation ("SRA"), its wholly-owned subsidiary, and Triton, a company that SRA entered into a joint venture with to work on the relevant government contract, alleging that the defendants violated the False Claims Act through various forms of government contract fraud. The relator worked for a defense contractor that was formerly subcontracted to work on a government contract with the defendants. The relator alleged that the defendants fraudulently induced the government into entering into the contract by employing a "bait and switch" method, concealing their insolvency, and misrepresenting the relator's expertise as their own. Additionally, the relator contends that the defendant charged excessive pass-through fees, made false statements in monthly status reports, created a kickback scheme, and misrepresented key information including overtime and direct labor charges, travel expenses, and personnel identities. The defendants moved to dismiss all of relator's claims for failure to state a claim under Rule 12(b)(6) and failure to plead fraud with particularity pursuant to Rule 9(b), and additionally argued that the relator's complaint was barred by the FCA's statute of limitations and that the relators failed to comply with the FCA's pre-filing requirements.

The court granted the defendants' motion to dismiss in large part, and denied it in part. First, the court determined that the relator's allegations were not barred by the statute of limitations because the amended complaint addressed the same underlying fraud as the original complaint, and thus related back to the original complaint, which was filed within the statute of limitations. Second, the court concluded that the relator met the FCA's pre-filing requirements, as the complaint was only unsealed once the government declined to intervene. Third, the court concluded that all of the relator's fraudulent inducement allegations failed because he did not adequately allege that the defendants actually made misrepresentations. Fourth, the court found that the relator sufficiently pled his fraudulent overtime billing claims against Triton by alleging that a discrepancy existed between Triton's actual overtime hours and overtime hours billed, identifying a specific time period in which the fraud occurred, and identifying specific invoices containing misrepresentations. However, the court granted SRA's motion to dismiss the overtime claims against it, explaining that the realtor failed to allege that SRA took any improper action related to overtime charges and also did not allege that SRA had knowledge of overtime misrepresentations. Fifth, the court determined that the relator failed to sufficiently allege that the defendants misrepresented travel expenses, as he did not allege who made the misrepresentations, when they were made, which defendants were involved, and did not identify any instance in which the defendants billed the government for the difference between the travel expense maximum and actual incurred travel costs. Sixth, the court dismissed the relator's fraudulent direct labor invoice allegations, finding that the relator did not explain or provide a statutory or regulatory authority explaining how the alleged lack of detail resulted in a false statement. The court also found that the relator's excessive pass-through fee allegations failed because his allegations were based on regulations that were not effective at the time the contract was awarded. Seventh, the court found that relator's kickback scheme allegations failed because the relator did not allege any underlying false claims and did not demonstrate how the defendant's coding system actually rendered false claims under the FCA. Additionally, the court concluded that the relator's falsely stated personnel identity allegations failed because the relator did not explain how the replacement of personnel was material to the government's payment decision or how the relator possessed standing to bring the claim, as the relator acknowledged it was a breach of contract dispute. Finally, the court found that the relator's false monthly status reports claims survived the defendants' motion to dismiss because the relator identified with requisite specificity invoices that contained alleged misrepresentations.

U.S. ex rel. Uhlig v. Fluor Corp., 2016 WL 5905714 (7th Cir. Oct. 11, 2016)

> **Holding: The U.S. Court of Appeals for the Seventh Circuit affirmed the district court's decision to grant the defendant's motion for summary judgment on the relator's government contracting false certification and retaliation allegations.**

The relator brought a *qui tam* suit against his former employer, a government contractor that provided electrical engineering services to the the United States Army, alleging that the defendant knowingly breached its contract with the government by employing unlicensed journeyman electricians and then submitting false invoices for their work, in violation of the False Claims Act. Additionally, the relator alleged that the defendant terminated his employment in retaliation for emailing his concern that the defendant was violating the contract terms to a website dedicated to defense contractor fraud. The U.S. District Court for the Central District of Illinois granted the defendant's motion for summary judgment on both the relator's FCA and retaliation claims, explaining that the defendant's contract did not require journeyman electricians to possess licenses and that the relator was not engaged in protected activity, as he did not have an objectively reasonable basis for his allegations. The relator appealed to the Seventh Circuit.

The circuit court affirmed the district court's decision, explaining that the defendant did not breach its contract because the contract language clearly stipulated that the defendant could establish an employee's qualifications outside of licensure, thus the relator could not establish falsity. The court also explained that the relator was not engaged in protected activity because he did not demonstrate that a reasonable employee in his position would have believed that the defendant violated the FCA because the relator did not review the contract language, thus he could not have known what the defendant's obligations were under the contract.

See U.S. ex rel. Beauchamp v. Academi Training Ctr., Inc., 2016 WL 7030433 (E.D. Va. Nov. 30, 2016) at page 32.

C. Reverse False Claims

U.S. ex rel. Harper v. Muskingum Watershed Conservancy Dist., 842 F.3d 430 (6th Cir. Nov. 21, 2016)

> Holding: The U.S. Court of Appeals for the Sixth Circuit affirmed the district court's decision to dismiss the relator's reverse false claims allegations, finding that the relator failed to state a claim for which relief could be granted under Rule 12(b)(6).

The relators brought a *qui tam* suit against an entity that was deeded an area of government land, alleging that the defendant violated the reverse false claims provision of the False Claims Act by violating their deed requirement to use the land only for "recreation, conservation, or reservoir-development purposes." Specifically, the relators alleged that the defendant violated these restrictions by selling rights to begin a hydraulic fracturing operation on the land. The U.S. District Court for the Northern District of Ohio granted the defendant's motion to dismiss the relator's allegations. The court found that the relators failed to demonstrate how the defendant knowingly took action to avoid its obligation to the government. The relators appealed to the Sixth Circuit.

The circuit court affirmed the district court's decision to grant the defendant's motion to dismiss. The court explained that the relators did not allege facts that created an inference that the defendant was aware of its violation of deed restrictions or that the defendant acted in "deliberate ignorance" or "reckless disregard." The court remarked that, "[a]lthough there is little established case law, given that Congress only recently amended the reverse-false-claim provision, the term 'knowingly' must be interpreted to refer to a defendant's awareness of *both* an obligation to the United States *and* his violation of that obligation. Because the relators have not pleaded facts that show such awareness, the district court properly dismissed their 'reverse' false claim." Additionally, the circuit court found that the relators only reached conclusory allegations that the defendants violated the FCA's conversion provision by delivering "less than all" of the government's property, as the relators failed to allege facts demonstrating that the defendants were aware or knew the title to the property presently belonged to the government or that they were violating deed restrictions.

U.S. ex rel. Customs Fraud Investigations, LLC. v. Victaulic Co., 2016 WL 5799660 (3rd Cir. Oct. 5, 2016)

> Holding: The U.S. Court of Appeals for the Third Circuit reversed and remanded the district court's decision to dismiss the relator's reverse false claims allegations with prejudice.

The relator, a limited liability company made up of former insiders from the pipe fitting industry, brought a *qui tam* suit against the defendant, a global manufacturer and distributor of pipe fittings, alleging that it avoided paying required marking duties by systematically importing millions of pounds of improperly marked pipe fittings without disclosing the improper markings to the government, in violation of the reverse false claims provision of the False Claims Act. The relator alleged that its principals had worked on numerous pipe and tube trade investigations and were able to uncover the alleged fraudulent scheme through an analysis of the defendant's shipping manifest data and studying the defendant's secondary market through eBay. The U.S. District Court for the Eastern District of Pennsylvania granted the defendant's motion to dismiss for failure to state a claim under Rule 12(b)(6) with prejudice, finding that the reverse false claims provision did not encompass a failure to pay marking duties. The relator promptly moved for leave to amend, including a First Amended Complaint that contained far more specific details regarding its fraud allegations. The district court denied the relator's motion for leave to amend, finding that the relator unduly delayed its motion for leave to file an amended complaint, and that the relator's amendment would be futile because the failure to pay marking duties could not, as a matter of law, give rise to reverse false claims liability. The relator appealed to the Third Circuit.

The circuit court reversed and remanded the district court's decision. The court found that the relator did not delay its motion for leave to file an amended complaint, explaining that the defendant's motion to dismiss and judges' questions and comments during oral argument did not put the relator on notice that the court would grant the motion to dismiss. The court observed that the relator filed promptly once the court granted the defendant's motion, which was all that was required. Further, the circuit court reversed the district court's holding that amendment would be futile, explaining that the failure to pay marking duties could potentially create FCA liability, as post-FERA statutory language, legislative history, and public policy all indicated that knowingly avoiding marking duties gives rise to FCA liability. The court also held that the relator's complaint met the requirements of Rule 9(b), explaining that it provided voluminous records, detailed methodology, and supporting expert opinions to sufficiently support its claims. The court also instructed the district court that upon remand, they must determine an appropriately limited discovery plan to diminish excessive expense based on the relator's allegations.

See *Hamilton v. Yavapai Cmty. Coll.*, 2016 WL 7102973 (D. Ariz. Dec. 6, 2016) at page 69.

D. Fraudulent Inducement

U.S. ex rel. Miller v. Weston Educ., Inc., 2016 WL 6091099 (8th Cir. Oct. 19, 2016)

Holding: The U.S. Court of Appeals for the Eighth Circuit reversed and remanded the district court's decision to grant the defendant summary judgment on the relator's fraudulent inducement allegations, and affirmed the district court's decision to dismiss one of the relator's retaliation claims.

The relators brought a *qui tam* suit against the for-profit college where they were formerly employed, alleging that it violated the False Claims Act by making false promises to the Department of Education ("DOE") in its Program Participation Agreement ("PPA") that it would maintain accurate student records. Specifically, the relators alleged that the defendant changed grades and attendance records for the sole purpose of obtaining funding and avoiding refunding DOE funds if a student withdrew or failed to obtain "satisfactory progress." Additionally, one of the relators alleged retaliation under the FCA, claiming that the defendant excluded her from meetings, removed her from her position as program manager, refused a previously-offered position, docked pay, and threatened termination. The U.S. District Court for the Western District of Missouri granted the defendant summary judgment on all claims. The relator appealed to the Eight Circuit solely on the theory of fraudulent inducement, arguing that the defendant's pattern of changing records indicated that when signing the PPA it did not intend to keep accurate records and that this false promise was material to the DOE's decision of whether or not to fund the defendant.

The circuit court reversed and remanded the district court's decision to grant the defendant summary judgment on the relators' FCA allegations and affirmed its decision with respect to the retaliation claims. The court found that the relators' evidence that both the defendant's internal policy and federal regulation emphasized accurate record keeping, in conjunction with the defendant's pattern of pre-PPA and post-PPA record falsification created a triable issue as to whether the defendant intended to comply with the PPA and how the defendant understood its record keeping obligations. Moreover, the court found that the relators showed that the alleged violations were material because the language of the relevant statute and the PPA, which conditioned payment on compliance with Title IV regulations, would cause a reasonable person to place importance on the promise of accurate record keeping and reporting. Finally, the court affirmed the district court's decision to dismiss the retaliation claims, finding that the relator provided insufficient support to prove that she was retaliated against.

E. False Certification of Compliance

U.S. ex rel. Williams v. City of Brockton, 2016 WL 7429176 (D. Mass. Dec. 23, 2016)

> **Holding: The U.S. District Court for the District of Massachusetts granted the defendants' motion to dismiss the relator's retaliation claims, but denied the defendants' motion to dismiss the relator's other allegations (that the defendant falsely certified compliance with civil rights and antidiscrimination laws in order to receive grants) for failure to state a claim under Rule 12(b)(6) and failure to plead fraud with particularity under Rule 9(b). The court also held that the relator's claims were not barred by the statute of limitations or the public disclosure bar.**

The relator brought a *qui tam* action against the city and police department where he was formerly employed as a police officer, alleging that the defendants violated the False Claims Act by obtaining grants through falsely certifying compliance with civil rights and anti-discrimination laws. Specifically, the relator alleged that the defendants engaged in an "ongoing pattern and practice" of discrimination against residents and employees, with disparate impact on minority residents, by failing to provide a multilingual website, and violated the "non-supplanting" conditions of their grant by unlawfully reducing the number of sworn officers. Additionally, the relator alleged that the defendants violated the anti-retaliation provision of the FCA by terminating the relator in response to his complaints about the defendants' alleged misconduct. The defendants moved to dismiss the relator's claims, arguing that he failed to state a claim under Rule 12(b)(6), failed to plead fraud with particularity under Rule 9(b), and was unable to overcome the public disclosure bar and the FCA's statute of limitations.

The court denied the defendant's motion to dismiss except as to the relator's retaliation claims. Applying the "holistic" approach to determining materiality, the court concluded that the relator sufficiently alleged materiality on the other claims, finding that the relator demonstrated that compliance with civil rights laws was a "central tenet" and "core value" of the program, providing strong evidence that the government would not have awarded the grants to the defendants if it had known of the their noncompliance. The court also found that the relator alleged scienter and falsity on these claims, explaining that the relator demonstrated that defendants "knew or should have known" that their conduct had a discriminatory impact on residents and employees. The court also held that the relator met the particularity requirements of Rule 9(b) by identifying several claims for payment. The court concluded that the relator's allegations fell within the FCA's statute of limitations because there was no reason that a government official with the responsibility to act knew or should have known of the misconduct prior to the relator's initial complaint. Additionally, the court rejected the defendant's argument that the relator's claims should be barred because they were based on publicly available newspaper articles, website documents, and grant recipient lists. The court ruled that the information contained in these documents was not substantially similar to the facts underlying relator's claims, and that the relator brought new allegations to light and allegations that "significantly differ in scope and kind." The court granted the defendants' motion to dismiss the relator's retaliation claims, finding that the relator did not engage in protected activity under the FCA because he alleged only that he was investigating misrepresentations made to the public, not to the government.

U.S. ex rel. Schneider v. J.P. Morgan Chase, 2016 WL 7408826 (D.D.C. Dec. 22, 2016)

Holding: The U.S. District Court for the District of Columbia granted the defendant's motion to dismiss the relator's claims that the defendant failed to comply with required servicing terms under HAMP.

The relator brought a *qui tam* suit against his mortgage loan servicer, alleging that the defendant violated the False Claims Act by falsely certifying compliance with servicing standards delineated in the National Mortgage Settlement and falsely certifying that it met the servicing standards specified in the Home Affordable Modification Program ("HAMP"). The defendant moved to dismiss the relator's claims for failure to state a claim under Rule 12(b)(6) and failure to plead fraud with particularity pursuant to Rule 9(b).

The court granted the defendant's motion to dismiss. The court found that the relator was required to exhaust the alternate dispute procedures laid out in the National Mortgage Settlement before filing his complaint. Additionally, the court found that relator failed to allege that the defendant's HAMP certifications were false, explaining that the defendant's misconduct had no "material effect on [the defendant's] ability to comply with the Making Home Affordable program."

U.S. ex rel. Escobar v. Universal Health Servs., 842 F.3d 103 (1st Cir. Nov. 22, 2016)

Holding: The U.S. Court of Appeals for the First Circuit reversed and remanded the district court's decision to grant the defendant's motion to dismiss relator's implied false certification claims for failure to state a claim under Rule 12(b)(6).

The relators brought a *qui tam* action against the defendant, a mental health facility treating the relators' daughter, alleging that the defendant violated the False Claims Act by falsely certifying that its employees were qualified to provide mental health treatment in order to receive payments from government healthcare programs. The relators alleged that the defendant billed the government for services using codes reserved for "professional staff member[s]" regardless of the staff's actual qualifications.

Additionally, the relators alleged that 22 of the defendant's employees used fake National Provider Identification numbers to misrepresent their status as social workers or licensed mental health counselors and that the defendant prescribed medication without the required supervision of a board-certified psychiatrist. The U.S. District Court for the District of Massachusetts dismissed relators' claims, finding that the relators failed to state a claim under the implied certification theory, as the defendant's false certifications did not violate an explicit condition of payment. The relators appealed to the U.S. Court of Appeals for the First Circuit, which reversed the district court's decision, finding that the defendant's violations were material conditions of payment. The defendant was granted certiorari from the Supreme Court and the Court concluded that the implied certification theory of liability could be a basis for a FCA claim, and vacated and remanded the decision for consideration of whether the defendant's alleged violations were material to the government's payment decision.

The circuit court reaffirmed its decision to reverse and remand the district court's decision to grant the defendant's motion to dismiss. Using the holistic approach laid out by the Supreme Court, the circuit court found that the relators sufficiently alleged that the defendant made material misrepresentations because the relators demonstrated that regulatory compliance was a relevant condition of payment, the licensing and supervision requirements of the facility go to the "very essence of the bargain," and the defendant's contractual relationships with Medicaid providers showed that compliance was influential on the government's payment decision. Moreover, the court noted that the government's effort to implement a series of regulations ensuring that mental health professionals were qualified to treat patients further supported the conclusion that the defendant's violations were material to the government's payment decision. Finally, the court rejected the defendant's argument that the government's continued payment after it was aware of the violations showed that compliance was not material, "mere awareness of allegations concerning noncompliance with regulations is different from knowledge of actual noncompliance."

U.S. ex rel. Beauchamp v. Academi Training Ctr., Inc., 2016 WL 7030433 (Nov. 30, 2016 E.D. Va.)

> **Holding: The U.S. District Court for the Eastern District of Virginia denied the defendant's motion to dismiss the relators' allegations of false claims stemming from false certifications of employee qualifications.**

The relators brought a *qui tam* suit against their former employer, a private security company providing protective security services to U.S. government officials in Afghanistan, alleging that the defendant submitted false reports and fraudulently billed the government for services provided by defendant's security personnel. The relators alleged that the defendant falsely certified that the security personnel passed the contractually required weapon qualifications test when in reality, they often failed the tests or were not properly tested at all. They alleged that the defendant fabricated test scores to submit fake scorecards to the government in order to receive payment for the security services under the government contract. The defendant moved for judgment on the pleadings under Rule 12(c), arguing that the relators failed to properly allege their false certification claims under the standard announced by the Supreme Court in *Universal Health Services v. U.S. ex rel. Escobar*.

The court denied the defendant's motion to dismiss, finding that the relators sufficiently alleged that the defendant made "specific representations" to the government that were false. The court explained that the billing codes and job titles contained in the invoices submitted to the government, when viewed in conjunction with the contract, specifically represented to the government that the defendant's personnel were properly qualified when they actually were not. Additionally, the court found that the defendant's argument that the relators must allege facts demonstrating that the government's payment decision would likely or actually have been influenced if it knew of the defendant's incompliance was "meritless because it requires leaving common sense at the door." The court explained that it "strains credulity to argue that the government's payment decision would not have been affected had the government known that the [employees] responsible for protecting U.S. officials in Afghanistan had not fulfilled the weapons qualifications requirement."

U.S. ex rel. Nelson v. Sanford-Brown, Ltd., 2016 WL 6205746, (7th Cir. Oct. 24, 2016)

> **Holding: The U.S. Court of Appeals for the Seventh Circuit found its prior dismissal of the relator's allegations of false certification of compliance with an educational institution's Program Participation Agreement comported with the Supreme Court's ruling in *Universal Health Services v. U.S. ex rel. Escobar*.**

The relator brought a *qui tam* suit against the for-profit educational institution where he was formerly employed as the Director of Education, alleging that the defendant violated the False Claims Act by falsely certifying compliance with the U.S. Department of Education's Title IV Program Participation Agreement ("PPA") requirements in order to obtain federal funding. The relator alleged that the defendant violated the regulations by causing its students to submit false requests for loans and grants and engaged in incentive-based compensation for admissions recruiters. In light of its ruling in *Universal Health Services v. U.S. ex rel. Escobar*, The U.S. Supreme Court remanded for reconsideration the U.S. Court of Appeals for the Seventh Circuit's previous affirming the U.S. District Court for the Eastern District of Wisconsin's dismissal of the relator's claims for determination of whether the defendant's false certifications were material to the government's payment decision.

The circuit court affirmed its prior decision, explaining that the relator's allegations amounted only to speculation, as he did not independently establish materiality and failed to provide evidence demonstrating that the defendant made any representations in connection with its claims for payment. The court noted that the relator failed to provide evidence of materiality to the government's payment decision that could overcome the contrary evidence that the defendant's subsidizing agency and other federal agencies that examined the defendant's conduct did not issue administrative penalties or termination.

U.S. v. Dynamic Visions, Inc., 2016 WL 6091099 (D.D.C. Oct. 24, 2016)

> **Holding: The U.S. District Court for the District of Columbia granted the government's motion for summary judgment on allegations that the defendants billed for unauthorized care in part.**

The relator brought a *qui tam* suit against a home-health care provider and its owner alleging that the defendants violated the False Claims Act by submitting claims to Medicaid for services that were not authorized by a "plan of care" signed by a physician or other qualified healthcare worker, or were authorized with forged or untimely signatures. The relator supported her allegations with the defendant's written agreement to comply with Medicare regulations, testimony from the Medicaid Director of the District of Columbia indicating that proper authorization was central to the Medicaid reimbursement decision, and a FBI review of the defendant's patient files. The relator moved for summary judgment.

The court granted the relator's motion for summary judgment in part and denied it in part. The court found that the relator's forgery allegations could not be supported without supplemental affidavits from physicians. However, the court found no genuine dispute that the defendant made impliedly false claims. The court first explained that the undisputed evidence demonstrated that the defendants withheld information about their regulatory violations and that they were on notice of the importance of complying with the regulations and their obligation to report violations because they entered into a Medicaid Provider Agreement which spelled out the requirements. Additionally, the court indicated that the relator's testimonial evidence from the Medicaid Director of the D.C. Medicaid Program stating that compliance with these regulations was the only way Medicaid could determine whether services were medically reasonable was sufficient to demonstrate that the defendant's conduct was material to Medicaid's payment decision. Further, the court observed that the defendant's records and preparation of an employee Medicaid compliance manual indicated that the defendant was at least reckless in not knowing that its violations were material to Department of Health Care Finance's payment. The court also noted that the evidence showed many records were missing plans of care and proper documentation and signature, and that "even a cursory review" of the files would have led the defendants to the conclusion that the records were not in compliance with the relevant regulations.

See *U.S. ex rel. Johnson v. Golden Gate Nat'l Senior Care, LLC*, 2016 WL 7197373 (D. Minn. Dec. 9, 2016) at page 49.

F. Incentive Compensation Ban

U.S. ex rel. Rose v. Stephens Inst., 2016 WL 5076214 (N.D. Cal. Oct. 28, 2016)

> **Holding:** The U.S. District Court for the Northern District of California granted the defendant's motion to certify the court's order denying its motion for summary judgment with respect to the relators' incentive compensation ban allegations for interlocutory appeal, citing the Supreme Court's recent ruling in *Universal Health Services v. U.S. ex rel. Escobar.*

The relators brought a *qui tam* action against an educational institution alleging that the defendant fraudulently obtained funds from the Department of Education ("DOE") by falsely certifying compliance with Title IV's incentive compensation ban ("ICB") in violation of the False Claims Act. The court denied the defendant's motion for summary judgment. However, the court also narrowed the relator's claims to a singular implied false certification claim. In light of the Supreme Court's ruling in *Universal Health Services v. U.S. ex rel. Escobar*, the defendant moved for reconsideration, arguing that the relator's allegations failed *Universal Health's* two-part test for falsity and that the ICB was not material under the test articulated in *Universal Health*. The court held that *Universal Health* did not stipulate a two part test, and that *Universal Health* did not affect the Ninth Circuit's holding in *Hendow*, thus, compliance with the ICB remained material to the government's payment decision and summary judgment was not warranted. The defendant moved to certify the aforementioned order for interlocutory appeal for four questions: (1) "whether *Universal Health's* 'two conditions' are necessary conditions for liability"; (2) "whether a failure to comply with the ICB automatically causes a loss of institutional eligibility"; (3) whether *Hendow* remains good law; and (4) given the DOE's past practice, have *Universal Health's* materiality standard has been met.

The court certified the defendant's motion for interlocutory appeal on all of defendants' questions except whether *Universal Health's* materiality standard was satisfied considering the DOE's past practice, explaining that the question was not a "question of law." The court noted that the remaining questions were suitable for interlocutory appeal, as the question of whether *Universal Health* created a two-part test for falsity was treated differently among the district courts and the remaining questions constituted issues of law on which reasonable jurists could disagree.

G. Medicaid Fraud

U.S. v. Dynamic Visions, Inc., 2016 WL 7115946 (D.D.C. Dec. 6, 2016)

> **Holding: The U.S. District Court for the District of Columbia granted the government's motion for summary judgment on its allegations that a home health care provider and its owner submitted false claims to Medicaid for reimbursement.**

The government brought an action under the False Claims Act alleging that a home health care provider and Isaiah Bongam, its sole owner and president, submitted claims to the government for reimbursement on services that did not comply with applicable regulations. The government alleged that the defendants failed include "plans of care" in patient files or included plans of care in patient files that were not signed by qualified health care workers or were signed with forged signatures.

The court granted the government's motion for summary judgment. The court observed that the government offered the declarations of FBI agents who participated in the fraud investigation and that the declarations provided undisputed evidence that the defendant submitted claims containing forged plans of care. Additionally, the court found that due to Bongam's ownership interest in the corporation and the commingling of his personal funds with those of the company, a sufficient degree of unity existed to pierce the corporate veil and hold Bongam liable.

U.S. ex rel. Ruckh v. CMC II LLC, 2016 WL 7665187 (M.D. Fla. Dec. 1, 2016)

> **Holding: The U.S. District Court for the Middle District of Florida denied the defendant's motion for summary judgment on relator's Medicare and Medicaid billing fraud claims.**

The relator brought a *qui tam* suit against the operator of skilled nursing facilities where she was formerly employed, alleging that the defendant violated the False Claims Act by fraudulently billing Medicaid and Medicare. The relator alleged that the defendant fraudulently overstated the amount of therapy that it administered to patients, misrepresented patients' medical conditions, and falsified records in order to obtain inflated reimbursements from the government. The defendant moved for summary judgment, primarily arguing that the relevant regulations were not in effect during the alleged time period, the relevant regulations served only as a condition of participation, and the relator relied on unreliable expert testimony.

The court denied the defendant's motion for summary judgment. After noting the relator's complaint provided little evidence, conclusory allegations, and lacked quantification, the court concluded that the defendant failed to demonstrate that there was no issue of material fact. The court explained that if the realtor's testimony was assumed admissible, it provides "at least somewhat more than no evidence," which created some issue of material fact.

H. Off-Label Marketing

U.S. ex rel. Brown v. Celgene Corp., 2016 WL 7626222 (C.D. Cal. Dec. 28, 2016)

> **Holding: The U.S. District Court for the Central District of California granted in part and denied in part the defendant's motion for summary judgment on the relator's off-label marketing and kickback allegations.**

The relator brought a *qui tam* suit against the pharmaceutical company where she was formerly employed in sales, alleging that the defendant engaged in off-label promotion of two cancer drugs, causing false claims to be submitted in violation of the False Claims Act. The relator also alleged that the defendant paid illegal kickbacks to physicians through speaker fees, paid clinical trials, advisory board positions, and authorship of ghost-written articles in exchange for prescribing and recommending the drugs, and caused claims tainted by those AKS violations to be submitted to the government in violation of the FCA. The defendant moved for summary judgment, arguing that (1) the relator could not demonstrate that the defendant's marketing campaign caused off-label prescriptions and (2) that the relator's claims were precluded by the FCA's six year statute of limitations.

The court granted in part and denied in part the defendant's motion for summary judgment. The court explained that the relator presented "sufficiently detailed circumstantial evidence" connecting false claims to the defendant's marketing campaign by demonstrating that claims for off-label prescriptions were submitted to the government following the defendant's promotions and that the physicians who received more promotional contacts prescribed the drugs at a greater rate than their counterparts with fewer contacts. Next, the court concluded that any claim submitted to Medicaid for non-medically accepted use was false because it was "statutorily ineligible for reimbursement." Further, the court held that the defendant's false statements were material, explaining that the requirement that the drugs were prescribed for medically accepted indications was an "essential feature" central to the functioning of the Medicare program. Moreover, the court rejected the defendant's argument that it could not possess the required scienter for liability under the FCA because its interpretation of the Medicare rules was "objectively reasonable." The court explained that all guidance and statutory text clearly communicated that medically unaccepted uses were not reimbursable, and pointed out that the defendant itself gave multiple presentations communicating this standard. However, the court granted the defendant's motion for summary judgment on the relator's AKS claims, observing that the relator failed to present evidence to show that the defendant's payments to physicians were excessive or that the amount the physicians were paid was tied to the volume of prescriptions they wrote. Finally, the court rejected the defendant's argument that the relator's claims were barred by the statute of limitations, explaining that although the relator knew of the alleged fraudulent conduct for many years before she filed her *qui tam* action, she would not have had reason to know that the conduct was illegal because the defendant had assured her that its actions were lawful.

JURISDICTIONAL ISSUES

A. Section 3730(b)(5) First-to-File Bar

U.S. ex rel. Palmieri v. Alpharma, Inc., 2016 WL 7324629 (D. Md. Dec. 16, 2016)

> **Holding: The U.S. District Court for the District of Maryland granted the defendants' motion to dismiss the relator's off-label marketing allegations, finding that the claims were barred by the FCA's first-to-file rule.**

The relator brought a *qui tam* suit against the pharmaceutical manufacturer where he was formerly employed as a sales representative, alleging that the defendant violated the False Claims Act by promoting off-label prescribing of its pain relief skin patch. Four days before the relator filed his complaint, a suit containing allegations regarding the same fraudulent scheme was filed and remained pending when the relator first filed suit. The U.S. District Court for the District of Maryland initially dismissed the relator's claims with prejudice for failure to plead fraud with particularity under Rule 9(b). On appeal, the U.S. Court of Appeals for the Fourth Circuit reversed and remanded to the district court, concluding that the district court erred in dismissing the relator's complaint with prejudice under Rule 9(b) without addressing whether the relator's claims were barred by the first-to-file rule or public disclosure bar.

The district court found that the relator's claims were barred by the first-to-file rule. The court explained that because the case filed prior to the relator's suit alleged the same material facts and was pending when the relator's case was filed, the relator's claims were precluded by the first-to-file bar. The court noted that because the first-filed case had been dismissed, the relator could refile.

B. Section 3730(e)(4) Public Disclosure Bar and Original Source Exception

U.S. ex rel. Solomon v. Lockheed Martin Corp., 2016 WL 7188298 (N.D. Tex. Dec. 12, 2016)

> **Holding: The U.S. District Court for the Northern District of Texas granted the defendants' motion for summary judgment on public disclosure grounds.**

The relator brought a *qui tam* action against a government defense contractor and the subcontractor where he was formerly employed as a compliance review specialist, alleging that the defendants conspired to conceal cost overruns on their defense contract with the government by misrepresenting their cost estimates and performance reports. While employed, the relator reported the alleged conduct to the Defense Contract Management Agency ("DCMA") and assisted with the DCMA investigation into his allegations. The DCMA and Government Accountability Office ("GAO") released reports detailing the alleged violations. After the relator completed his work on the defense contract, he received an internal memorandum that supported his allegations, but did not disclose the memorandum to the government while employed with the defendant. Once retired, the relator continued to alert the government about the defendants' alleged misrepresentations and forwarded the memorandum to a senator and the GAO. The defendants moved for summary judgment on all of the relator's claims, arguing that his claims were precluded by the public disclosure bar and that he was not an original source of his claims.

The court granted the defendants' motion for summary judgment. The court found that the relator's allegations were publicly disclosed in the DCMA and GAO reports. Additionally, the court concluded that the relator was not an original source because, while the relator reported the fraud to the government before bringing his suit, his disclosure was not "voluntary" as required by the FCA because the terms of his employment obligated him to report fraud to the government. The court observed that the relator's employer's contract with the government required it to report fraud to the government, and thus the relator had an affirmative duty to report the fraud to the government due to his position in compliance. The court noted that the information the relator disclosed when no longer working for the company, including the internal memorandum, was insufficient to overcome the bar because it only reiterated his previous disclosure, and "once a relator involuntarily provides information, he may not subsequently voluntarily provide the same information."

U.S. ex rel. Silver v. Omnicare, Inc., 2016 WL 6997010 (D.N.J. Nov. 28, 2016)

> **Holding: The U.S. District Court for the District of New Jersey granted the defendants' motion for summary judgment on the relator's kickback allegations, finding that the relator's allegations were precluded by the public disclosure bar and the relator did not qualify as an original source.**

The relator brought a *qui tam* suit against two long-term care pharmacies alleging that the defendants engaged in a kickback scheme in which they offered drugs prices below market value to nursing homes in exchange for Medicare Part D or Medicaid prescription referrals. The relator based his claims on his experience in the nursing home and pharmacy business, though he never worked for either of the defendants. He allegedly discovered the kickback scheme by reading several public publications on the industry. He alleged that he deduced that the defendants engaged in illegal swapping arrangements that violated the Anti-Kickback Statute and submitted false claims to the government that were tainted by the AKS violations in violation of the False Claims Act after reading online financial information that he claimed showed the defendants were selling drugs below market value. The defendants moved for summary judgment, arguing that the relator's allegations were precluded by the public disclosure bar.

The court granted the defendants' motion for summary judgment. The court explained that "the information cumulatively disclosed in the publicly available documents was sufficient to support an inference that [the defendants] allegedly engaged in swapping transactions…" The court rejected the relator's arguments that "the revenue side" was unknown and that he independently supplied specific dollar figures, noting that during the relator's deposition he stated the opposite, indicating that he did not need to know the "individual costs and prices" or any non-publicly disclosed information in order to conclude that the defendant engaged in a swapping scheme. Finally, the court concluded that the relator did not qualify as an original source because he did not materially add to the publicly disclosed information.

State of New York ex rel. Khurana v. Spherion Corp., 2016 WL 6652735 (S.D.N.Y. Nov. 10, 2016)

> **Holding: The U.S District Court for the Southern District of New York granted the defendant's motion to dismiss the relator's implied certification allegations related to Anti-Kickback Statute violations finding that the public disclosure bar precluded the relator's allegations, the relator failed to plead fraud with particularity under Rule 9(b), and failed to state a claim under Rule 12(b)(6). The court also found that the defendant was not vicariously liable for its consultants' fraudulent activity.**

The relator brought a *qui tam* suit against his former employer, a corporation contract-ed by New York City's Office of Payroll Administration ("OPA") to provide quality assurance over the OPA's automated time-keeping and payroll function project. The relator alleged that the defendant made multiple false certifications that the project would succeed as planned and that all subcontracts were made without conflicts of interest, and that the defendant violated the Anti-Kickback Statute and submitted tainted claims in violation of the False Claims Act. The relator also alleged that the defendant terminated the relator in retaliation for raising concerns about the proj-ect's failure and potential fraud. Further, the relator alleged that because consultants working for the defendant participated in fraudulent billing and awarded contracts to family or friends in exchange for kickbacks the defendant was vicariously liable for the actions of the consultants. In addition to filing suit, the relator mailed his allegations to the New York City Department of Investigations ("DOI") and posted information to CNN's online citizen journalism forum. He also met with DOI investigators and provided a flash drive of information which he alleges was not available in any pub-lic sources. Alongside the relator's efforts, the New York media covered the alleged conduct, causing the Office of the Comptroller of the City of New York to audit the defendant corporation's oversight on the project and publish a report. Shortly after, a criminal complaint against the consultants was unsealed and a federal grand jury is-sued an indictment. The defendant moved to dismiss arguing that the relator's claims were precluded by the public disclosure bar and that the relator failed to state a claim under Rule 12(b)(6) and failed to plead with particularity pursuant to Rule 9(b).

The court granted the defendant's motion to dismiss with respect to all allegations except relator's retaliation claims. The court explained that the criminal complaint, re-port, and media coverage qualified as public disclosures and that the disclosures were substantially similar to the relator's allegations, as they set forth the essential elements of the relator's vicarious liability claims and provided sufficient information to put the government on notice of potential fraudulent activity. The court determined that the relator was not an original source of his claims because the disclosures he made to the government before filing suit did not reference the fraudulent kickback or overbilling schemes, but only referenced the project's failure. Additionally, the court found that the information the relator provided in his disclosures was vague or conclusory and his complaint did not materially add to the already publically disclosed material. The court also found that the relator failed to state a claim under Rule 12(b)(6) because he did not adequately allege that the defendant failed to provide quality assurance services or that it provided an incorrect description to the government. Furthermore, the court explained that the relator failed to allege an implied false certification theory, as he did not identify specific misrepresentations or "misleading half-truths" made by the defendant. Next, though the court found the relator's fraudulent billing allegations plausible, it concluded that the relator failed to plead fraud with sufficient particular-ity, as he did not identify who was involved in submitting claims, what the claims re-garded, when they were submitted, and also did not offer identifying information for submitted or false claims. Finally, the court denied the defendant's motion to dismiss

the relator's retaliation claims, finding that the relator plausibly alleged he was terminated as a result of voicing concerns and that the defendant was aware of his protected
conduct.

U.S. ex rel. Saldivar v. Fresenius Med. Care Holdings, Inc., 2016 WL 841 F.3d 927 (11th Cir. Nov. 8, 2016)

**Holding: The U.S. Court of Appeals for the Eleventh Circuit re-
versed and remanded the district court's decision, finding that the
relator's claims were precluded by the public disclosure bar because he did not qualify as an original source of his allegations of
overfill billing violations.**

The relator brought a *qui tam* action against an End Stage Renal Disease outpatient
services provider where he was formerly employed as chief technician, alleging that the
defendant violated the False Claims Act by billing the government for the overfill in its
drug vials, a practice that allegedly violated CMS billing statutes. The relator alleged
these violations based on his personal experience monitoring the use of overfill in conjunction with inter-employee conversations and corporate policies. The U.S. District
Court for the Northern District of Georgia concluded that while the allegations at the
basis of the relator's action were publically disclosed, the relator qualified as an original
source due to his experience with the relevant drugs' inventory, discussions related to
overfill use and billing with supervisors and coworkers, and his knowledge of the defendant's corporate policy. However, the district court granted the defendant summary
judgment, finding that although claims submitted were false, the defendant did not
possess the required intent. The relator appealed to the Eleventh Circuit.

The circuit court reversed and remanded the district court's decision. The circuit
court explained that the district court was correct in concluding that the allegations at
the basis of the relator's suit were publically disclosed in various public sources and it
was clear that the government was aware of the defendant's billing practices. However,
the circuit court found that the district court erred in concluding that the relator was
an original source of his claims, explaining that the relator's direct and independent
knowledge only related to administration and inventory, but did not give relator direct insight into price-related contracts or any other pricing and billing information.
Furthermore, the court determined that the information that relator gained from coworker conversations was indirect.

U.S. ex rel. Pospisil v. Syngenta AG, 2016 WL 5851795 (D. Kan. Oct. 6, 2016)

> **Holding: The U.S. District Court for the District of Kansas granted the defendant's motion to dismiss, finding that the relator could not qualify as an original source and failed to plead fraud with particularity pursuant to Rule 9(b).**

The relator, a corn farmer, brought a *qui tam* action against the manufacturer of genetically-modified corn alleging that the commercialization of its products depressed the corn market, causing the government to pay millions of dollars in crop insurance claims that it otherwise would not have paid in violation of the False Claims Act. Specifically, the relator contends that the defendant's commercialization caused its genetically-modified corn to comingle within the larger United States' corn supply, which led to China refusing all corn imports due to the presence of genetically-modified seeds, consequently lowering corn prices and economically harming farmers. The defendant moved to dismiss the relator's claims for failure to state a claim under Rule 12(b)(6) and failure to plead fraud with particularity under Rule 9(b). The defendant also moved to dismiss on public disclosure grounds, arguing that the relator's claims were publically disclosed in news articles reporting on the thousands of similarly situated plaintiffs who filed class-action suits against the defendant based on the same allegations.

The court granted the defendant's motion to dismiss. The court found that the relator's claims were precluded by the public disclosure bar and that the relator was not an original source. The court rejected the relator's argument that meetings he had with the defendant to discuss its plan to isolate the genetically-modified corn, in which the relator allegedly told the defendant that the plan was a "fraud" which would not work, qualified him as an original source because he provided evidence of the defendant's scienter that materially added to the publicly disclosed allegations. The court explained that the relator's allegations only added detail to the "universe of allegations" that were already publically disclosed in the class action suits. Moreover, the court found that the relator failed to plead fraud with particularity under Rule 9(b) because he failed to allege how any crop insurance claim was false, identify a specific false statement associated with a crop insurance claim, or point to a source of duty for farmers who submitted crop insurance claims. Finally, the court noted that the relator failed to plead a plausible claim of causation because he did not allege any affirmative steps taken by the defendant to submit actual false claims.

See U.S. ex rel. Proctor v. Safeway, Inc., 2016 WL 7017231 (C.D. Ill. Dec. 1, 2016) at page 62.

FALSE CLAIMS ACT
RETALIATION CLAIMS

U.S. ex rel. Salters v. American Family Care, Inc. 2016 WL 7242180 (N.D. Ala. Dec. 15, 2016)

> **Holding: The U.S. District Court for the Northern District of Alabama denied the defendant's motion for partial summary judgment on the relator's retaliation claim.**

The plaintiff brought a retaliation action under the False Claims Act against the medical care provider where she was formerly employed, alleging that the defendant improperly terminated her in retaliation for her protected whistleblowing activity. The plaintiff alleged that she raised concerns that the defendant's practice of billing for laboratory tests ordered by a physician who was not actually in the clinic violated the FCA. The defendants moved for partial summary judgment, arguing that they had a non-retaliatory basis to terminate the plaintiff.

The court denied the defendants' motion for partial summary judgment. The court concluded that the plaintiff demonstrated the first two elements of a *prima facie* retaliation case, as her email to the president regarding potential violations qualified as protected activity and her termination qualified as an adverse employment action. Further, the court explained that the close temporal proximity between her protected activity and her termination demonstrated that the events could be related, particularly because the executive who ultimately terminated the relator was aware of her protected activity and terminated her only six weeks after she raised concerns. Lastly, the court found that though the defendants offered a non-retaliatory reason for the plaintiff's termination, the plaintiff presented sufficient evidence that the proffered non-retaliatory reason was pretextual to allow the case to proceed.

Steele v. Great Basin Sci., Inc., 2016 WL 6839384 (D. Utah Nov. 21, 2016)

> **Holding: The U.S. District Court for the District of Utah granted the defendant's motion to dismiss the plaintiff's retaliation claims for failure to state a claim under Rule 12(b)(6).**

The plaintiff brought a retaliation claim under the False Claims Act against the diagnostic blood pathogen testing kit manufacturer where she was formerly employed alleging that the defendant terminated her in retaliation for attempting to stop FCA violations by raising concerns about potential testing kit contamination. The defendant moved to dismiss the plaintiff's allegations for failure to state a claim under Rule 12(b)(6).

The court granted the defendant's motion to dismiss. The court found that the plaintiff's activity was not protected under the FCA because she only attempted to improve the quality of the defendant's products and did not put the defendant on notice that she was preparing a *qui tam* suit or preventing fraud. The court rejected the plaintiff's argument that because her complaints were unrelated to her job as the director of recruitment, her employer was put on notice of a potential suit, explaining that the plaintiff did not allege in the complaint that her job was unrelated to regulating the facility's contamination and that acting outside of one's stated duties is insufficient to put an employer on notice. Additionally, the court noted that the defendant did not submit any requests for payment to the government, and it would be "less than apparent" that the defendant would be liable under the FCA for knowingly selling substandard products that may eventually be purchased by the government.

Drumm v. Triangle Tech, Inc., 2016 WL 6822422 (M.D. Penn. Nov. 18, 2016)

> **Holding: The U.S. District Court for the Middle District of Pennsylvania granted the defendant's motion to dismiss two of the four plaintiffs' retaliation claims for failure to state a claim under Rule 12(b)(6).**

The plaintiffs brought retaliation claims against the technical school where they were formerly employed, alleging that the defendant terminated two plaintiffs, Joseph Drumm and Ronald McElwee in retaliation for attempting to stop False Claims Act violations and terminated the remaining plaintiffs, Carol Beck and Lisa Delbaugh, due to their well-known close personal relationship with Drumm and McElwee. The plaintiffs alleged that the defendant asked Drumm produce false documents to allow disbursement of government funds, but that he refused and contacted his supervisor and the vice president of human resources. They alleged that Drumm reported the request to the Department of Education ("DOE") and met with McElwee and the Office of the Inspector General ("OIG") to investigate the defendant. The OIG concluded that the defendant wrongfully received $70,000, which was returned to the DOE to resolve the issue. However, the plaintiffs alleged that soon after the defendant discovered that Drumm and McElwee met with the OIG, the defendant closely monitored the four relators performance and terminated the under false pretenses. The defendant moved to dismiss the plaintiffs' allegations for failure to state a claim under Rule 12(b)(6).

The court granted the defendant's motion to dismiss with respect to Beck and Delbaugh, explaining that they failed to allege that they took action in furtherance of a *qui tam* suit. The court found that Drumm and McElwee sufficiently demonstrated that they engaged in protected activity by contacting the DOE and meeting with the OIG. The court rejected Beck and Delbaugh's argument that they were protected through the "zone of interest" theory due to their close friendships with Drumm and

McElwee, indicating that they did not cite any authorities supporting the extension of the theory to friendship.

U.S. ex rel. Herman v. Coloplast Corp., 2016 WL 7042191, (D. Minn. Nov. 9, 2016)

> **Holding: The Magistrate Judge in the U.S. District Court for the District of Minnesota recommended that the court grant the defendant's motion for summary judgment on relators' retaliation claims, finding that the relators' allegations were barred by their Separation Agreements and the FCA's statute of limitations.**

The relators brought a *qui tam* action against their former employer, a ostomy and continence care product manufacturer, alleging that the defendant terminated them in retaliation for their investigation of and refusal to participate in an alleged fraudulent scheme that provided illegal kickbacks to suppliers in exchange for switching to the defendant's products, in violation of the False Claims Act's retaliation provisions. While employed by the defendant, the relators signed an Employment Agreement that dictated severance terms, and at the time of termination the relators signed a Separation Agreement that included their severance packages and an agreement not to bring claims related to their employment against the defendant in any form, excluding claims that arise after the date of the Separation Agreement. The defendant moved to dismiss the relators' allegations for failure to state a claim under Rule 12(b)(6), or in the alternative, for summary judgment, arguing that the relators' claims were nullified by their Separation Agreements and were time-barred.

The court recommended that the court grant the defendant's motion for summary judgment. The court rejected the relators' argument that the Separation Agreement was a prospective and thus void as against public policy, explaining that the releases only applied to claims "up to the date" they were signed. The court noted that the relators' argument that the Separation Agreements ran contrary to the FCA and public policy was misplaced because the releases did not foreclose the relators from bringing substantive *qui tam* actions, but only from bringing retaliation claims, which the court determined were related to the relators' employment only. The court explained that the "FCA retaliation claims…[were] personal to the individual employee" and that the releases had "no impact on the *qui tam* claims." Lastly, the court concluded that the relator's retaliation claims were also time-barred because they only appeared in the amended complaint filed after the statute of limitations had passed for retaliation claims and the claims did not relate back to or arise from the original complaint.

Scates v. Shenandoah Memorial Hosp., 2016 WL 6270789 (W.D. Va. Oct. 26, 2016)

> **Holding: The U.S. District Court for the Western District of Virginia granted the defendant's motion for summary judgment on the relator's retaliation claims, finding that the relator was not engaged in protected activity and the defendant provided a legitimate reason for termination.**

The plaintiff brought a retaliation action under the False Claims Act against a medical imaging facility where she was formerly employed as an ultrasound technician, alleging that the defendant terminated her in retaliation for reporting her concern that the defendant was engaged in fraudulent billing. The relator alleged that the defendant's technicians took fewer ultrasound photos than billing standards required. The defendant moved for summary judgment, arguing that the relator's belief that the defendant was committing fraud was objectively unreasonable.

The court granted the defendant's motion for summary judgment, finding that the relator was not engaged in protected activity because she did not demonstrate an objectively reasonable belief that the defendant was committing fraud. The court noted that the relator only alleged that the defendant underbilled the government, which was not a violation of the FCA, and that the relator's concerns were based on a general conversation about the industry that she overheard and then applied to her employer. The court explained that the defendant's claims that it terminated the relator due to poor coworker relationships, history of workplace conflict, and refusal to change her behavior during a performance improvement plan were acceptable non-retaliatory reasons.

See *U.S. ex rel. Complin v. N.C. Baptist Hosp.*, 2016 WL 7471311 (M.D.N.C. Dec. 28, 2016) at page 61.

See *U.S. ex rel. Williams v. City of Brockton*, 2016 WL 7429176 (D. Mass. Dec. 23, 2016) at page 30.

See *U.S. ex rel. Uhlig v. Fluor Corp.*, 2016 WL 5905714 (7th Cir. Oct. 11, 2016) at page 26.

COMMON DEFENSES TO
FCA ALLEGATIONS

A. Not Knowingly False

U.S. ex rel. Johnson v. Golden Gate Nat'l Senior Care, LLC, 2016 WL 7197373 (D. Minn. Dec. 9, 2016)

> **Holding: The U.S. District Court for the District of Minnesota denied in part the defendants' motion for summary judgment on the relator's claims of false certification of compliance with Medicare therapy regulations.**

The relators, an occupational therapist and her employer, brought a *qui tam* suit against a rival provider of nursing home therapy services and the nursing homes where the individual relator was formerly employed, alleging that the defendants violated the False Claims Act by falsely certifying compliance with Medicare's statutory and regulatory requirements for physical and occupational therapy. The relator alleged that the defendants billed for services provided by unlicensed therapists, failed to ensure proper supervision, did not properly document therapy provided, mischaracterized the monitoring of group therapy, billed for therapy that was not actually provided, failed to accurately track and record therapy time, and provided services without a physician-certified plan of care. The defendants moved for summary judgment.

The court denied in part the defendants' motion for summary judgment. The court determined that the relators provided sufficient evidence to create a dispute of material fact as to their unlicensed therapy claims, group therapy monitoring allegations, and allegations that the defendants billed for services that were not provided. Additionally, the court denied the defendants' motion to dismiss the relators' supervision allegations, rejecting the defendants' argument that the relevant requirements were ambiguous. Further, the court denied summary judgment on the relators' skilled therapy services allegations concluding that a jury should hear scientific expert testimony to interpret the term "skilled services" as used in the regulations. The court granted the defendants' motion as to the documentation related claims, finding that the defendants' interpretation of the Medicare regulations was objectively reasonable and the relators failed to provide evidence that the defendants knew their documentation practices were not in compliance with Medicare regulations. The court also granted the defendants' motion as to the relators' inaccurate time keeping allegations, finding that the relators asserted the theory only upon learning new information through discovery. Finally, the court granted the defendants' motion on the relators' improper certification claims, explaining that the relators did not specifically plead these allegations in their amended complaints.

See *U.S. ex rel. Ruscher v. Omnicare, Inc.*, 2016 WL 6407128 (5th Cir. Oct. 28, 2016) at page 21.

B.   Sovereign Immunity

O'Connell v. Regents of the Univ. of California, 2016 WL 6872948 (9th Cir. Nov. 22, 2016)

> **Holding: The U.S. Court of Appeals for the Ninth Circuit affirmed the district court's dismissal of the relator's claims against a state entity.**

The relator filed a *qui tam* action against the governing board of The University of California, alleging that the defendant violated the False Claims Act. The U.S. District Court for the Northern District of California dismissed the relator's action, finding that the university was a state entity immune from suit under the FCA. The relator appealed to the Ninth Circuit.

The circuit court affirmed the district court's dismissal. The court explained that the defendant was a state entity and therefore the relator did not have a statutory basis under the FCA to file a private action against it.

U.S. ex rel. Guardiola v. Renown Health, 2016 WL 6803078 (D. Nev. Nov. 15, 2016)

> **Holding: The U.S. District Court for the District of Nevada denied the relator's motion for leave to file a third amended complaint against the government for a share of an alternate remedy, finding that the False Claims Act does not waive sovereign immunity.**

The relator brought a *qui tam* suit against a medical center alleging that the defendant violated the False Claims Act by improperly billing government-funded health insurance programs. The relator settled her suit and filed a joint stipulation of dismissal with the defendant, but alleged that after declining to intervene, the government pursued some of the claims brought in her FCA suit through a Recovery Audit Contract ("RAC"). The relator filed suit, arguing that she was entitled to a share of the recovery because the RAC constituted an "alternate remedy." The U.S. District Court for the District of Nevada found that because the United States declined to intervene in the *qui tam* action, it was not a party in the suit and the court lacked jurisdiction. Subsequently, the relator moved for leave to file a third amended complaint in order to add the United States as a party. The United States did not respond, but moved for leave to file an *amicus curiae* brief in opposition, arguing that granting leave to amend would be futile as sovereign immunity would bar any claim the relator brought against the United States.

The court denied the relator's motion for leave to file a third amended complaint. First, the court determined that the United States' motion to file an amicus brief was improper because it was an opposing party. Next, the court rejected the relator's argument that the FCA waived sovereign immunity by granting the relator a share of the government's direct or alternate remedy recovery. The court explained that the FCA did not waive sovereign immunity because there was no statutory text that explicitly allowed a relator to bring a suit against the United States in order to recover an alternate remedy.

C. Employment Agreements

U.S. ex rel. Welch v. My Left Foot Children's Therapy, LLC, 2016 WL 5867410 (D. Nev. Oct. 6, 2016)

> **Holding: The U.S. District Court for the District of Nevada denied the defendant's motion to stay pending the outcome of its appeal on its motion to compel arbitration.**

The relator brought a *qui tam* action against her former employer, a provider of children's speech and physical therapy, alleging that the defendant violated the False Claims Act by charging government insurance programs for medically unnecessary services. The relator entered into an employment agreement wherein she agreed to arbitrate claims stemming from her employment by the defendant. The defendant moved to compel arbitration and the U.S. District Court for the District of Nevada denied the defendant's motion. The defendant then filed a motion to stay pending their appeal of the court's denial of its motion to compel arbitration, or in the alternative, pending the decision on its motion to dismiss.

The court denied the defendant's motion to stay. The court explained that the defendant did not demonstrate that it was likely to succeed on the merits of the motion to compel arbitration because the government was the real party in interest and the defendant could not compel the government to arbitrate, as it did not agree to the arbitration agreement. Additionally, the court observed that defendant failed to demonstrate that it would be irreparably injured without a stay, noting that the only harms it alleged were the monetary harms of discovery and filing a motion to dismiss, which would occur anyway during arbitration. Finally, the court determined that granting the defendant's motion to stay would be unfair to the relator and would not serve the public interest.

See *U.S. ex rel. Herman v. Coloplast Corp.*, 2016 WL 7042191, (D. Minn. Nov. 9, 2016) at page 47.

D. Issue Preclusion

U.S. ex rel. Lockey v. City of Dallas, 2016 WL 5794745 (5th Cir. Oct. 4, 2016)

Holding: The U.S. Court of Appeals for the Fifth Circuit affirmed the district court's decision, finding that the relator's housing false certification claims were barred largely by issue preclusion.

The relators filed a *qui tam* suit against the defendant city of Dallas and its Housing Authority, alleging that the defendants violated their federal civil rights obligations, namely their obligation to affirmatively further fair housing, but submitted claims for federal funding containing false certifications that they had met those obligations in violation of the False Claims Act. The U.S. District Court for the Northern District of Texas granted the defendants' motion for summary judgment on these claims, finding that the public disclosure bar precluded the relators' claims. On appeal, the Fifth Circuit affirmed the district court's decision. The relators subsequently filed a new action in which the district court granted defendant's motion to dismiss holding that the realtors' suit was barred by issue preclusion and the public disclosure bar. The relator appealed to the Fifth Circuit.

The circuit court affirmed the district court's decision, agreeing that the realtors' new action only restated their previous claims more narrowly and therefore their allegations were barred by issue preclusion.

E.   Failure to Prove Falsity

U.S. ex rel. Zeman v. Univ. of S. Cal., 2016 WL 6407409 (9th Cir. Oct. 31, 2016)

> **Holding: The U.S. Court of Appeals for the Ninth Circuit affirmed the district court's decision to grant the defendant's motion for summary judgment on the relator's Medicare overbilling allegations with prejudice.**

The relator brought a *qui tam* suit against a university hospital alleging that it violated the False Claims Act by double billing Medicare for its overhead costs and improperly coding services. The U.S. District Court for the Central District of California granted the defendant's summary judgment and the realtor appealed to the Ninth Circuit.

The circuit court affirmed the district court's dismissal, finding that there was no evidence that the relator's allegations constituted violations of Medicare requirements. Specifically, the court noted that the defendant's billed facility fees fell within Medicare's guidelines and the relator did not provide sufficient support for her remaining claims.

F.   Corporate Structure

U.S. ex rel. Bunk v. Gov't Logistics N.V., 842 F.3d 261, (4th Cir. Nov. 15, 2016)

Holding: The U.S. Court of Appeals for the Fourth Circuit reversed and remanded the district court's decision to grant summary judgment on the relator's successor corporation liability claims, finding that the relator successfully pled a theory of fraudulent transaction.

The relators brought a *qui tam* suit against two companies that ship household goods and belongings under a government contract with the Department of Defense ("DOD"), alleging that the defendants conspired to implement a bid-rigging scheme that would allow them to substantially increase the prices that the DOD paid for shipping, in violation of the False Claims Act. The U.S. District Court for the Eastern District of Virginia entered a verdict in favor of the government and the relators, but denied the relators a recovery of civil penalties against one of the defendants' purported corporate successors. On appeal, the U.S. Court of Appeals for the Fourth Circuit remanded to determine whether the relator could recover from the successor corporation of a defendant. The district court dismissed the relators' claims against the successor corporation and awarded the defendant summary judgment, finding that the relators' claims were inadequately pled, and in the alternative, rejected them on the merits, finding that there was insufficient evidence of successor liability to justify a trial. The relator appealed to the Fourth Circuit.

The circuit court vacated and remanded the district court's decision. The circuit court explained that the relator satisfied Rule 9(b), as it sufficiently outlined the relationship between the two companies and solidly alleged a theory of fraudulent transaction resulting in successor liability. The circuit court confirmed that the district court could exercise supplemental jurisdiction over the successor corporation, reasoning that the relators' claims were not part of a new lawsuit. Next, the circuit court examined the viability of relators' two theories—the substantial continuity theory and the fraudulent transaction theory of successor liability. The circuit court concluded that the district court was correct in not applying the substantial continuity test, as the FCA does not reference successor corporation liability and therefore did not impact the common law principles regarding successor corporation liability. However, the circuit court determined that the district court erred in concluding that the relators did not form a solid foundation for their fraudulent transaction theory, explaining that the two companies' service agreements, employment methods, and business interest purchases all sufficiently outlined a relationship between the two corporations that satisfied fraudulent transaction theory. Moreover, the complaint detailed that the successor corporation viewed itself as a continuation of the initial corporation and the initial corporation continued to gain profit from previous contracts. Additionally, the circuit court determined that the district also erred in awarding summary judgment to the defendant, explaining that the crux of fraudulent transaction theory rested on the intention underlying the transfer of assets, and "the issue of fraudulent intention is generally not amendable to resolution on summary judgment." In this case, the court concluded that the evidence could not only "dispel the requisite fraudulent intention," but also could "establish it," and then identified several "badges of fraud" in the complaint that could lead a reasonable juror to conclude fraudulent intent, these included inadequacy of consideration, unusual transactions, transactions anticipating suit or execution, or transactions in which the debtor benefits.

U.S. ex rel. Scollick v. Narula, 2016 WL 6078246 (D.D.C. Oct. 17, 2016)

> **Holding: The U.S. District Court for the District of Columbia granted the defendant's motion to dismiss the relator's allegations that the defendant made false statements to the government to obtain government contracts for failure to state a claim upon under Rule 12(b)(6) and failure to plead fraud with particularity pursuant to Rule 9(b) in part and denied it in part.**

The relator brought a *qui tam* suit against the several construction companies and individual defendants alleging that the defendants conspired to violate the False Claims Act and its reverse false claims provision by fraudulently obtaining and then failing to return government funds awarded through construction contracts specifically set aside for businesses with statuses that the defendants did not possess. The relator alleged that individual defendants Neil Parekh, Vijay Narula, and Ajay Madan created Centurion Solutions Group ("CSG") as a front company to gain service-disabled veteran-owned small business ("SDVOSB") status by falsely using defendant Amar Gogia—a service-disabled veteran—as chief owner and controller, falsely certifying details about CSG's past performance, and falsifying employee information. Furthermore, the relator alleged that Parekh falsely certified defendant Citibuilders as an SDVOSB and executed a similar conspiracy with defendant KCGI, Inc. Finally, the relator alleged that the defendant insurance companies also violated the FCA by issuing bonds for the defendants' contracts despite awareness of the details within the defendants' bid proposal. The defendants moved to dismiss the relator's claims for failure to state a claim under Rule 12(b)(6) and failure to plead fraud with particularity pursuant to Rule 9(b).

The court granted the defendants' motion to dismiss in part. First, the court found that the relator's application of the alter ego doctrine to allege vicarious liability between the defendants only amounted to a legal conclusion because the relator failed to identify any facts that demonstrated "comingling, manipulation, and diversion," a lack of formalities in individual relationships, how two individuals could be alter egos of one another, or most importantly, how an inequitable result followed by failing to pierce the corporate veil. Second, the court explained that CSG, Citibuilders, and KCGI were the only defendants liable for making false claims, presenting false claims, or conspiring because the relator failed to sufficiently allege the alter ego doctrine and failed to allege that the remaining defendants played a substantial role in the submission of false claims. Additionally, the court noted that the relator failed to demonstrate that the insurance defendants caused the submission of false claims merely by issuing bonds because the relator did not allege any facts indicating that the insurance defendants agreed to issue bonds in furtherance of fraud or continued to do business with the other defendants once aware of false claims. Third, the court determined that the relator failed to allege his reverse false claims allegations with sufficient particularity against all defendants, explaining that the relator failed to identify an obligation to return payment to the government. Fourth, the court explained that because the relator alleged "time, place, content, and recipients" of false claims in conjunction with nine specific allegedly fraudulent contracts, the relator plead with sufficient particularity that defendants Parekh and Citibuilders, conspired to make and present false claims to the government. The court rejected Citibuilders use of the intracorporate conspiracy doctrine to argue that the conspiracy claim should be dismissed because the alleged conspiracy was executed "through its own directors, officers, and employees," finding that because the relator alleged conspiracy between all defendants, reliance on the intracorporate conspiracy doctrine was unavailing. Finally, the court determined that the relator sufficiently stated his claim that individual defendants Narula and Madan played a substantial role in the submission of false claims, as they established CSG as a front company in order to obtain SDVOSB status, were directly responsible in preparation of CSG bid proposals, and identified Gogia as the owner to obtain fraudulent funding.

G.   Statute of Limitations

U.S. ex rel. Walker v. Loving Care Agency, Inc. 2016 WL 7408848 (D.N.J. Dec. 22, 2016)

> **Holding: The U.S. District Court for the District of New Jersey denied the defendant's motion to dismiss the relators' Medicaid fraud claims for failure to plead fraud with particularity under Rule 9(b). The court granted the defendant's motion to dismiss some claims as time barred.**

The relators brought a *qui tam* suit against the for-profit homecare agency where they were formerly employed as registered nurses, alleging that the defendant defrauded Medicaid in violation of the False Claims Act. Specifically, the relators alleged that they witnessed the defendant submitting claims to Medicaid for services that were never performed, not properly supervised, medically unnecessary, administered to family members, provided to ineligible beneficiaries, and performed by unqualified individuals as a result of defendant's fraudulent training program. The defendant moved to dismiss the relators' claims for failure to plead fraud with sufficient particularity pursuant to Rule 9(b) and argued that some of the relators' claims were barred by the FCA's statute of limitations.

The court denied the defendant's motion in large part and granted the motion to dismiss some claims pursuant to the statute of limitations. The court found that the relators satisfied the particularity requirements of Rule 9(b), explaining that they provided either representative examples that sufficiently supported an inference that false claims were submitted, or listed multiple specific examples of false requests for reimbursement that identified patients, individual employees, and exact dates of the allegedly fraudulent services. The court also found that the relators properly alleged scienter by alleging that they informed their supervisors of the fraud. Furthermore, the court concluded that the relators sufficiently alleged that the defendant's fraudulent certifications were material, explaining that it would be "hard to fathom" that the alleged systematic, widespread scheme would be immaterial to the government's payment decision. Lastly, the court rejected the defendant's argument that all claims outside of the time period of the relators' employment should be dismissed, finding that the complaint alleged fraud with sufficient particularity as to the claims prior to their employment, and the relators maintained relationships with current employees who informed them that the fraudulent conduct is on-going. However, the court dismissed claims occurring six years prior to the complaint's filing date pursuant to the statute of limitations.

U.S. ex rel. Jackson v. Univ. of N. Tex., 2016 WL 720915 (5th Cir. Dec. 12, 2016)

Holding: The U.S. Court of Appeals for the Fifth Circuit affirmed the district court's decision to dismiss the relator's false certification claims on statute of limitations grounds.

The relator brought a *qui tam* suit against his former university and student loan issuers and processers, alleging that the defendants submitted false claims to the government for the relator's loan eligibility and disbursement. The government declined to intervene. The U.S. District Court for the Eastern District of Texas dismissed the relator's claims, finding that they were barred by the FCA's six year statute of limitations. The relator appealed to the Fifth Circuit.

The circuit court affirmed the district court's decision. The court explained that because the government declined to intervene, the six year statute of limitations applied to the relator's claims. The court rejected the relator's argument that he could take advantage of the ten year statute of limitations because he was acting as a government official when bringing his *qui tam* suit.

FEDERAL RULES OF CIVIL PROCEDURE

A. Rule 9(b) Failure to Plead Fraud with Particularity

U.S. ex rel. Complin v. N.C. Baptist Hosp., 2016 WL 7471311 (M.D.N.C. Dec. 28, 2016)

Holding: The Magistrate Judge for the U.S. District Court for the Middle District of North Carolina recommended that the court grant the defendants' motion to dismiss with prejudice the relator's retaliation claims and allegations that the defendants inflated their Medicare reimbursements claims.

The relator brought a *qui tam* suit against the hospital system where he was formerly employed an associate director, alleging that the defendants failed to disclose their employees' healthcare claims on their Medicare Cost Report, causing falsely increased reimbursements and an inflated Medicare "Wage Index" in their geographic area. Additionally, the relator alleged that he was fired in retaliation for his internal complaints about fraud. The defendants moved to dismiss the relator's complaint for failure to plead fraud with particularity under Rule 9(b) and failure to state a claim upon which relief can be granted under Rule 12(b)(6).

The Magistrate Judge recommended that the court grant the defendants' motion to dismiss the relator's claims with prejudice. The court concluded that the relator met the particularity requirements of Rule 9(b), noting that, contrary to the defendants' argument, the relator was not required to identify the names of officers who made the false statements on the cost reports, and that neither the FCA nor Rule 9(b) required the relator to possess personal knowledge of the alleged fraud. However, the court found that the relator failed to allege any evidence that could create an inference that the defendant possessed knowledge or awareness of the alleged misconduct. Moreover, the court rejected the relator's attempt to establish scienter by demonstrating recklessness through a failure to become aware of industry laws and regulations, by inferring "motive and opportunity" to defraud the government via complex employment benefit plans, or through allegations that the hospital claimed fictitious costs. Finally, the court determined that the relator failed to allege that the defendant took adverse employment action against him, as the time between the defendants' discovery of the relator's suit and the relator's termination was too great to satisfy the FCA's causation element. The court also found that the relator's proposed amendments failed to plausibly establish scienter or causation, warranting the dismissal of all relator's claims with prejudice.

U.S. ex rel. Driscoll v. Spencer, 2016 WL 7229135 (E.D. Cal. Dec. 14, 2016)

> **Holding: The U.S. District Court for the Eastern District of California granted the defendants' motion to dismiss the relator's inflated medical bill claims for failure to plead fraud with particularity pursuant to Rule 9(b) and failure to state a claim under Rule 12(b)(6).**

The relator brought a *qui tam* suit against the medical group and community hospital where he was formerly employed as a diagnostic radiologist, alleging that the defendants submitted fraudulent claims for unnecessary or unperformed radiology scans and procedures in violation of the False Claims Act. The relator alleged that the defendants falsely certified compliance with government healthcare regulations and submitted the false bills to the government. The defendants moved to dismiss the relator's complaint for failure to plead fraud with particularity under Rule 9(b) and failure to state a claim under Rule 12(b)(6).

The court granted the defendants' motion to dismiss the relator's claims. The court concluded that the relator failed to allege sufficient facts to demonstrate that the defendants expressly certified compliance with any law or regulation, who certified compliance, how it was certified, the relationship between compliance and funding, and whether and to what extent the false certifications caused defendants to receive payment that they otherwise would not have received.

U.S. ex rel. Proctor v. Safeway, Inc., 2016 WL 7017231 (C.D. Ill. Dec. 1, 2016)

> **Holding: The U.S. District Court for the Central District of Illinois denied the defendant's motion to dismiss the relator's claims that the defendant overbilled government healthcare plans by failing to report accurate "usual and customary" prices for failure to plead fraud with particularity under Rule 9(b) and failure to state a claim under Rule 12(b)(6). The court also found that the relator's claims were not precluded by the public disclosure bar.**

The relator, a licensed pharmacist, brought a *qui tam* suit against a nationwide grocery retailer and its pharmacy affiliates, alleging that the defendant caused the government to overpay for prescriptions through its healthcare programs by offering discounts to its customers through a membership program but failing to report those discounted prices to the government as "usual and customary" when seeking reimbursement. The defendant moved to dismiss the relator's claims, arguing improper venue, failure to plead fraud with particularity under Rule 9(b), and that the suit was precluded by the public disclosure bar.

The court denied the defendant's motion to dismiss. First, the court determined that the case was brought in the proper venue because the complaint alleged a nationwide scheme that was executed at numerous stores within the judicial district. Second, the court found that the relator met the particularity requirements of Rule 9(b), as he identified who submitted false claims, the nature of the fraud, the fraud's time period, where the fraud took place, and detailed how the fraud was executed. The court also found that the relator stated a claim under the FCA by alleging that because the defendant failed to offer the government the usual and customary price, the government did not get the benefit of its bargain with the defendant. The court also noted that the relator provided details of the alleged scheme along with representative examples. Lastly, the court determined that a second *qui tam* suit and a legal news report did not constitute a prior public disclosure. The court reasoned that even though the relator's amended complaint contained more detail after the second *qui tam* suit was filed, the relator's claims were not barred because he was the first to allege the relevant fraud claim. Moreover, the relator qualified as an original source because he acquired independent knowledge through his work in a pharmacy operating under the defendant's policies.

U.S. ex rel. Lawton v. Takeda Pharm. Co., Ltd., 842 F.3d 125 (1st Cir. Nov. 22, 2016)

Holding: The U.S. Court of Appeals for the First Circuit affirmed the district court's decision to dismiss the relator's off-label marketing and kickback allegations for failure to plead fraud with particularity under Rule 9(b).

The relator brought a *qui tam* suit against a competitor of the drug manufacturer where he was formerly employed, alleging that the defendant engaged in an illegal off-label marketing scheme and paid kickbacks to researchers to produce studies supporting the off-label uses for its drugs in violation of the Anti-Kickback Statute. The relator alleged that the defendant submitted claims tainted by the AKS violations to the government in violation of the False Claims Act. The U.S. District Court for the District of Massachusetts granted the defendant's motion to dismiss the relator's claims for failure to plead fraud with particularity pursuant to Rule 9(b). The relator appealed to the First Circuit.

The circuit court affirmed the district court's decision to dismiss the relator's claims for failure to meet the particularity requirements of Rule 9(b). The court concluded that the realtor failed to allege with specificity who submitted the false claims, the number of false claims submitted, and how the defendant's conduct resulted in false claims. Instead, the relator's complaint required the court to infer that government funds were used to pay unlawful claims merely from the relator's postulation that 30% of the drug's annual sales were for off-label prescriptions and the amount of government funds spent on the drug.

U.S. ex rel. Fisher v. IASIS Healthcare LLC, 2016 WL 6610675, (D. Ariz. Nov. 9, 2016)

Holding: The U.S. District Court for the District of Arizona denied the defendants' motion to dismiss the relators' allegations that the defendants submitted claims that purposefully bypassed medical necessity and cost-effectiveness review, and granted the defendants' motion to dismiss the relators' kickback and conspiracy allegations.

The relators brought a *qui tam* suit against a hospital management company and its wholly owned subsidiary that provided insurance to Medicaid beneficiaries, alleging that the defendants created a preferential program that violated the Anti-Kickback Statute ("AKS") and False Claims Act and caused claims to be submitted that were not medically necessary or cost effective. The relators also alleged that the defendants provided the government with data reports that were not complete or accurate, in violation of the defendants' contract with the government, but falsely certified that they had provided accurate reports. The relators alleged that the defendants gave preferential treatment to certain providers in exchange for keeping the providers in the defendants' network. Additionally, the relators alleged that the defendants did not properly credential providers, violated the government's performance standards through understaffing, and created a "place-holder" billing code that improperly allowed approval of blocks of claims at once. The defendants moved to dismiss the relators' claims for failure to state a claim upon which relief can be granted under Rule 12(b)(6) and for failure to plead fraud with particularity under Rule 9(b).

The court denied the defendants' motion to dismiss and granted it in part. The court determined that the relators failed to demonstrate how the defendants' preferential program resulted in financial gain for defendants, caused federal insurance programs to sustain financial loss, or could have an actual—not speculative—impact on the defendants' or government's financial results. Furthermore, the court explained that the relators' complaint failed to allege that the defendants' conduct fell outside the AKS safe harbor. However, the court found that the relators properly alleged their claims that the defendants improperly waived authorization, used block approvals, and failed to verify medical necessity or cost effectiveness. The court explained that the relators identified specific breaches in defendants' obligations to the government relating to medical necessity and cost-effectiveness, prior authorization, and credentialing. The court noted that the relators gave specific examples of claims approved with insufficient documentation, emails regarding compliance concerns, non-credentialed physicians, backdating of credentialing, and statistics. The court also concluded that the relators met the Supreme Court's materiality standard set out in *U.S. ex rel. Escobar v. Universal Health Services*, explaining that the relators alleged not only that the defendants breached their contract, but also that the contract's language indicated that the government would not have paid if it was aware of the defendants' practices.

U.S. ex rel. Whatley v. Eastwick College, 2016 WL 6311614 (3rd Cir. Oct. 28, 2016)

Holding: The U.S. Court of Appeals for the Third Circuit affirmed the district court's decision to dismiss the relator's allegations of educational fee and fund misrepresentation with prejudice for failure to meet the particularity requirements of Rule (9) and failure to state a claim under Rule 12(b)(6).

The relator brought a *qui tam* suit against the for-profit college where she was formerly enrolled, alleging that the defendant violated Title IV's incentive compensation ban by offering cash incentives to its recruiters, made false promises to students that their credits were transferrable, grossly inflated book and lab fees, manipulated students' federal aid to frontload fees without providing refunds for students who withdrew or failed, and arbitrarily assigned grades in violation of Title IV, all while falsely certifying compliance with Title IV requirements in violation of the False Claims Act. The relator also alleged on personal experience that the defendant claimed federal financial aid for her education after she withdrew from the institution by altering her attendance records. The U.S. District Court for the District of New Jersey granted the defendant's motion to dismiss for failure to meet the requirements of Rule 9(b) and failure to state a claim under Rule 12(b)(6). The relator appealed to the Third Circuit.

The circuit court affirmed the district court's decision. The court explained that the relator failed to state a claim under Rule 12(b)(6) regarding her allegations related to transferable credits, overcharges, a fees, because she failed to show that the defendant's actions violated any regulations or resulted in FCA liability, rather, the court indicated that the relator only alleged "conclusory assertions." The court first explained that the relator did not identify specific regulations that the defendant violated or any particular misrepresentations made with respect to book, lab, or other allegedly improper fees. Additionally, the court determined that the while the relator properly alleged that the defendant violated the incentive compensation ban, the relator failed to plead with particularity pursuant to Rule 9(b), as she did not provide information regarding who provided payments, to whom the payments were sent, or the criteria for payment. Moreover, the court explained that the relator's grade alteration allegations failed because the relator did not identify which individuals altered students' grades and which grades were altered. Finally, the court found that allegations based on relator's personal experience failed to meet the particularity requirements of Rule 9(b) because the relator did not specify who made misrepresentations or altered her attendance after her withdrawal.

U.S. ex rel. Schutte v. Supervalu, Inc., 2016 WL 6139913 (C.D. Ill. Oct. 21, 2016)

Holding: The U.S. District Court for the Central District of Illinois denied the defendants' motion to dismiss relators' claims that the defendants failed to report accurate "usual and customary" prices to the government for failure to state a claim under Rule 12(b)(6) and failure to plead fraud with particularity under Rule 9(b).

The relators, both former pharmacists, brought a *qui tam* suit against a nationwide retail grocery and pharmacy owner and its affiliates, alleging that through a uniform, nationwide policy in which their centralized pharmacy transaction information system reported inflated "usual and customary prices" to the government instead of the discounted prices that the defendant was actually offering to the general public, they systematically overcharged the government for prescription drugs in violation of the False Claims Act. The relators included examples of printouts of customer transactions from the information system, which they alleged demonstrated the difference between government-reported prices and actual discounted prices. The defendants moved to dismiss the relators' claims for failure to state a claim under Rule 12(b)(6) and failure to plead fraud with particularity under Rule 9(b).

The court denied the defendants' motion to dismiss. The court rejected the defendants' argument that the relators failed to meet the requirements of Rule 9(b) because they did not allege specific claims against each of the named defendants. The court explained that because the relators alleged fraud through the defendants' nationwide information system, their allegations provided all of the defendants with fair notice of the claims against them. Further, the court found that the relators properly alleged falsity and materiality, citing the defendants' annual certifications of accuracy and truthfulness of the reported drug prices. Lastly, the court noted that the relators' representative examples were sufficient to extrapolate a nationwide fraud scheme.

U.S. ex rel. Scollick v. Narula, 2016 WL 6078246 (D.D.C. Oct. 17, 2016)

Holding: The U.S. District Court for the District of Columbia granted the defendant's motion to dismiss the relator's allegations that the defendant made false statements to the government to obtain government contracts for failure to state a claim upon under Rule 12(b)(6) and failure to plead fraud with particularity pursuant to Rule 9(b) in part and denied it in part.

The relator brought a *qui tam* suit against the several construction companies and individual defendants alleging that the defendants conspired to violate the False Claims Act and its reverse false claims provision by fraudulently obtaining and then failing to return government funds awarded through construction contracts specifically set aside for businesses with statuses that the defendants did not possess. The relator alleged that individual defendants Neil Parekh, Vijay Narula, and Ajay Madan created Centurion Solutions Group ("CSG") as a front company to gain service-disabled veteran-owned small business ("SDVOSB") status by falsely using defendant Amar Gogia—a service-disabled veteran—as chief owner and controller, falsely certifying details about CSG's past performance, and falsifying employee information. Furthermore, the relator alleged that Parekh falsely certified defendant Citibuilders as an SDVOSB and executed a similar conspiracy with defendant KCGI, Inc. Finally, the relator alleged that the defendant insurance companies also violated the FCA by issuing bonds for the defendants' contracts despite awareness of the details within the defendants' bid proposal. The defendants moved to dismiss the relator's claims for failure to state a claim under Rule 12(b)(6) and failure to plead fraud with particularity pursuant to Rule 9(b).

The court granted the defendants' motion to dismiss in part. First, the court found that the relator's application of the alter ego doctrine to allege vicarious liability between the defendants only amounted to a legal conclusion because the relator failed to identify any facts that demonstrated "comingling, manipulation, and diversion," a lack of formalities in individual relationships, how two individuals could be alter egos of one another, or most importantly, how an inequitable result followed by failing to pierce the corporate veil. Second, the court explained that CSG, Citibuilders, and KCGI were the only defendants liable for making false claims, presenting false claims, or conspiring because the relator failed to sufficiently allege the alter ego doctrine and failed to allege that the remaining defendants played a substantial role in the submission of false claims. Additionally, the court noted that the relator failed to demonstrate that the insurance defendants caused the submission of false claims merely by issuing bonds because the relator did not allege any facts indicating that the insurance defendants agreed to issue bonds in furtherance of fraud or continued to do business with the other defendants once aware of false claims. Third, the court determined that the relator failed to allege his reverse false claims allegations with sufficient particularity against all defendants, explaining that the relator failed to identify an obligation to return payment to the government. Fourth, the court explained that because the relator alleged "time, place, content, and recipients" of false claims in conjunction with nine specific allegedly fraudulent contracts, the relator plead with sufficient particularity that defendants Parekh and Citibuilders, conspired to make and present false claims to the government. The court rejected Citibuilders use of the intracorporate conspiracy doctrine to argue that the conspiracy claim should be dismissed because the alleged conspiracy was executed "through its own directors, officers, and employees," finding that because the relator alleged conspiracy between all defendants, reliance on the intracorporate conspiracy doctrine was unavailing. Finally, the court determined that the relator sufficiently stated his claim that individual defendants Narula and Madan played a substantial role in the submission of false claims, as they established CSG as a front company in order to obtain SDVOSB status, were directly responsible in preparation of CSG bid proposals, and identified Gogia as the owner to obtain fraudulent funding.

See *U.S. ex rel. Walker v. Loving Care Agency, Inc.*, 2016 WL 7408848 (D.N.J. Dec. 22, 2016) at page 59.

See *U.S. ex rel. Hagerty v. Cyberonics*, 844 F.3d 26 (1st Cir. Dec. 16, 2016) at page 88.

See *Hamilton v. Yavapai Cmty. Coll.*, 2016 WL 7102973 (D. Ariz. Dec. 6, 2016) at page 69.

See *U.S. ex rel. Schaefer v. Family Med. Ctrs. of South Carolina*, 2016 WL 6601017 (D.S.C. Nov. 8, 2016) at page 70.

See *U.S. ex rel. Bingham v. HCA, Inc.*, 2016 WL 6027115 (S.D. Fla. Oct. 14, 2016) at page 22.

See *U.S. ex rel. Pospisil v. Syngenta AG*, 2016 WL 5851795 (D. Kan. Oct. 6, 2016) at page 44.

See *U.S. ex rel. Customs Fraud Investigations, LLC. v. Victaulic Co.*, 2016 WL 5799660 (3rd Cir. Oct. 5, 2016) at page 27.

B. Rule 12(b)(6) Failure to State a Claim upon which Relief Can Be Granted

Hamilton v. Yavapai Cmty. Coll., 2016 WL 7102973 (D. Ariz. Dec. 6, 2016)

> **Holding: The U.S. District Court for the District of Arizona denied in part the defendants' motion to dismiss the relator's claims related to fraudulent education funding for failure to state a claim under Rule 12(b)(6).**

The relator brought a *qui tam* suit against the community college where he was formerly employed and a flight school that ran the airplane program at the school, alleging that the defendants conspired to submit false claims to the Department of Veteran's Affairs ("VA") in order to obtain education benefit funding. Specifically, the relator alleged that the defendants knowingly and falsely represented compliance with the "85/15" rule, which required that no more than 85% of a program's students were federally financially supported. The relator alleged that the defendants employed several methods to falsely satisfy the 85/15 rule including counting ineligible students as "non-supported students," paying for non-veteran tuition only, participating in a scholarship program that targeted only students who would later become "non-supported," and improperly combining four independent programs into a single program when reporting. The relator also alleged that the defendants violated the reverse false claims provision of the FCA by failing to self-report their misconduct and return the fraudulent funding. The defendants moved to dismiss the relator's claims for failure to state a claim under Rule 12(b)(6).

The court denied the defendants' motion to dismiss all of relator's claims except the reverse false claims allegations. The court found that the relator adequately pleaded scienter by demonstrating through the defendants' own records, the text of the 85/15 rule, a warning from the VA that students needed to be admitted to be counted, and internal staff warnings that the defendants failed to meet their "duty to make a limited inquiry" that would have alerted them to the FCA violations. Furthermore, the court determined that the relator met the particularity requirements of Rule 9(b) by sufficiently demonstrating "the who, what, when, where, and how" of the fraud. The court also found that the relator adequately alleged conspiracy because the relator properly alleged that the defendants were a joint venture. However, the court granted the defendants' motion to dismiss the relator's reverse false claims allegations, finding that the relator failed to allege an obligation to pay the government.

U.S. ex rel. Schaefer v. Family Med. Ctrs. of South Carolina, 2016 WL 6601017 (D.S.C. Nov. 8, 2016)

> **Holding: The U.S. District Court for the District of South Carolina denied the defendants' motion to dismiss relator's Stark Law and improper billing allegations, finding that the plaintiffs sufficiently pled scienter and materiality and met the particularity requirements of Rule 9(b).**

In this intervened case, the plaintiffs alleged that a medical center violated the False Claims Act and Stark Law by engaging in employment arrangements that directly linked physician pay to volume or value of physician referrals and devised multiple improper billing schemes. Specifically, the plaintiffs alleged that the defendants programmed billing software to misrepresent services, used systematic billing practices that caused the submission of tens of thousands of medically unnecessary claims, and issued standing orders for non-routine tests regardless of medical need. The defendants moved to dismiss for failure to state a claim under Rule 12(b)(6) and for failure to plead fraud with sufficient particularity pursuant to Rule 9(b).

The court denied the defendants' motion to dismiss. The court found that the plaintiffs properly pled both scienter and materiality to establish the "who, what, where, when, and how" of the alleged FCA and Stark Law violations. Additionally, the court rejected the defendants' argument that the government's continued payment of the allegedly false claims showed that the false statements were not material to the government's payment decision, and concluded that "that the proper focus with respect to materiality is the influence of the false statement at the time of presentment."

U.S. ex rel. Whatley v. Eastwick College, 2016 WL 6311614 (3rd Cir. Oct. 28, 2016)

> **Holding: The U.S. Court of Appeals for the Third Circuit affirmed the district court's decision to dismiss the relator's allegations of educational fee and fund misrepresentation with prejudice for failure to meet the particularity requirements of Rule (9) and failure to state a claim under Rule 12(b)(6).**

The relator brought a *qui tam* suit against the for-profit college where she was formerly enrolled, alleging that the defendant violated Title IV's incentive compensation ban by offering cash incentives to its recruiters, made false promises to students that their credits were transferrable, grossly inflated book and lab fees, manipulated students' federal aid to frontload fees without providing refunds for students who withdrew or failed, and arbitrarily assigned grades in violation of Title IV, all while falsely certifying compliance with Title IV requirements in violation of the False Claims Act . The relator also alleged on personal experience that the defendant claimed federal financial aid for her education after she withdrew from the institution by altering her attendance records. The U.S. District Court for the District of New Jersey granted the defendant's motion to dismiss for failure to meet the requirements of Rule 9(b) and failure to state a claim under Rule 12(b)(6). The relator appealed to the Third Circuit.

The circuit court affirmed the district court's decision. The court explained that the relator failed to state a claim under Rule 12(b)(6) regarding her allegations related to transferable credits, overcharges, a fees, because she failed to show that the defendant's actions violated any regulations or resulted in FCA liability, rather, the court indicated that the relator only alleged "conclusory assertions." The court first explained that the relator did not identify specific regulations that the defendant violated or any particular misrepresentations made with respect to book, lab, or other allegedly improper fees. Additionally, the court determined that the while the relator properly alleged that the defendant violated the incentive compensation ban, the relator failed to plead with particularity pursuant to Rule 9(b), as she did not provide information regarding who provided payments, to whom the payments were sent, or the criteria for payment. Moreover, the court explained that the relator's grade alteration allegations failed because the relator did not identify which individuals altered students' grades and which grades were altered. Finally, the court found that allegations based on relator's personal experience failed to meet the particularity requirements of Rule 9(b) because the relator did not specify who made misrepresentations or altered her attendance after her withdrawal.

See *U.S. ex rel. Escobar v. Universal Health Servs.*, 842 F.3d 103 (1st Cir. Nov. 22, 2016) at page 31.

See *U.S. ex rel. Harper v. Muskingum Watershed Conservancy Dist.*, 842 F.3d 430 (6th Cir. Nov. 21, 2016) at page 27.

See *U.S. ex rel. Customs Fraud Investigations, LLC. v. Victaulic Co.*, 2016 WL 5799660 (3rd Cir. Oct. 5, 2016) at page 27.

LITIGATION DEVELOPMENTS

A. Calculating Damages and Civil Penalties

U.S. v. Luce, 2016 WL 6892857 (N.D. III. Nov. 23, 2016)

Holding: The U.S. District Court for the Northern District of Illinois granted the government's motion for summary judgment on damages and penalties for the defendant's defaulted loans and false certifications.

The government brought a suit under the False Claims Act against an attorney who owned a mortgage company that served as a loan correspondent for the Department of Housing and Urban Development ("HUD"), alleging that the defendant falsely certified compliance with HUD's annual verification form provision requiring that it had no employees that were involved in criminal proceedings. The defendant certified compliance with the provision despite being indicted for various frauds during the relevant time period. The U.S. District Court for the Northern District of Illinois granted the government's motion for summary judgment on liability and the government moved for summary judgment on penalties and damages.

The court granted the government's motion for summary judgment. First, the court reviewed the defendant's liability, recognizing that a reasonable person would attach importance to the certifications, and the defendant, having served as an attorney at the SEC, had reason to know that the government attached importance to his certifications. Additionally, the court explained that the "likely or actual behavior of the recipient" influenced the government's payment decision, noting that HUD disbarred the defendant upon discovering his false certifications. Next, the court determined that the government was permitted to recover damages because "but for" the defendant's false certifications, the government would not need to pay defaulted loans, as the defendant would not have been in the position to originate any loans. The court also noted that the defendant did not present any facts disputing the government's request for damages. Therefore, the court determined that the government's total award was $10,373,997.69 by calculating the collective loss on the refinanced loans and adding the FCA's minimum statutory penalty for the three verification forms he signed.

B.   Costs and Attorneys' Fees

U.S. ex rel. Emery v. Belcon Enter, Inc., 2016 WL 7494855 (D. Me. Dec. 30, 2016)

> **Holding: The Magistrate Judge for the U.S. District Court for the District of Maine recommended that the court grant in part the relator's motion for attorney's fees.**

The relator settled a *qui tam* suit under the False Claims Act and moved for an award of attorney's fees. Throughout the *qui tam* action, the relator was represented by two attorneys, one local and one out-of-state. The defendant raised multiple objections to relator's motion.

The Magistrate Judge recommended that the district court grant in part the relator's motion for attorney's fees. The court recommended deducting the total hours billed in response to the defendant's challenges to the out-of-state attorney's complaint composition, teleconferences, emailing, and associate work as excessive, duplicative, too vague, or unrecoverable. Additionally, in response to the defendant's arguments that the out-of-state attorney's travel time charges were ambiguous and that his rate should not exceed the local attorney's rate, the court reduced the out-of-state attorney's travel rate to half of the attorney's regular rate and reduced the out-of-state firms' rates to accord with the range of FCA hourly rates deemed reasonable in recent cases. Finally, the court rejected the defendant's argument that the relator's counsel could not charge for work on claims on which the relator did not prevail, but agreed with the defendant that all claims entitled "office work" were too vague to discern the necessity or reasonableness of the charge, and therefore should be excluded.

U.S. ex rel. Smith v. The Boeing Co., 2016 WL 7035001 (D. Kan. Dec. 2, 2016)

> **Holding: The U.S. District Court for the District of Kansas denied the defendant's motion for costs.**

The relator brought a *qui tam* suit against a government contractor alleging that the defendant defrauded the government in violation of the False Claims Act. The U.S. District Court for the District of Kansas granted the defendant summary judgment and the Tenth Circuit affirmed that decision. The defendant moved for costs.

The court denied the defendant's motion for costs. The court concluded that although the defendant was the prevailing party, the relator's undisputed indigence in conjunction with the difficult nature of the case warranted denial of the defendant's motion.

U.S. ex rel. Stephens v. Malik, 2016 WL 6818880 (N.D. Ind. Nov. 28, 2016)

Holding: The U.S. District Court for the Northern District of Indiana granted the relator's petition for attorney fees and expenses.

In this partially intervened case, the relator brought a *qui tam* suit against the physician defendant alleging that he violated the False Claims Act and Stark Law by referring Medicare patients to the medical care facility solely owned by his brother. The government settled the case with the defendant the relator petitioned for attorney's fees and expenses. The defendant challenged the requested amount, arguing that the fees should be reduced slightly because the amount of hours was unreasonable and the relator did not calculate the fees using his attorney's actual hourly rate.

The court granted the relator's petition. The court determined that, though the relator's attorney's rate increased during the litigation, it was permissible to apply the current rate retroactively. The court also found that the defendant's challenge to the number of hours was based on conclusory evidence and that the amount of hours was reasonable.

C. FCA Seal/Service Issues

U.S. ex rel. Meyn v. Citywide Mortgage Assoc., Inc., 2016 WL 7336415 (D. Kan. Dec. 19, 2016)

> **Holding: The U.S. District Court for the District of Kansas granted the defendant's motion to dismiss the relator's claims for failure to comply with the FCA's seal requirements.**

The relator brought a *qui tam* suit against a mortgage lending company, alleging that it violated the False Claims Act by ending the relator's refinancing process under a Veteran's Administration loan upon discovering that his residence was refinanced at a greater value than it was actually worth. The defendant moved to dismiss relator's claims, arguing that the relator's failure to comply with the FCA's seal requirement warranted dismissal.

The court granted the defendant's motion to dismiss. The court concluded that because the relator did not attempt to comply with the FCA's seal requirement in filing his complaint, dismissal was appropriate. Furthermore, the court concluded that regardless of the relator's noncompliance with the seal requirement, the court would dismiss relator's complaint for failure to state a claim under Rule 12(b)(6), as the relator failed to allege that the defendant received any payment from the government.

State Farm Fire and Casualty Co. v. U.S. ex rel. Rigsby, 137 S. Ct. 436 (Dec. 6, 2016)

> **Holding: The United States Supreme Court affirmed the Fifth Circuit's decision to deny the defendant's motion to dismiss, holding that violating the FCA seal requirement does not mandate dismissal.**

The relators, two claims adjusters employed by a contractor that provided disaster claims management services for the defendant, State Farm insurance company, brought a *qui tam* action alleging that the defendant submitted false claims to the government for payment on flood policies arising out of damage caused by Hurricane Katrina. Before the court lifted the seal, the relators' attorney disclosed the existence of the *qui tam* suit to multiple news outlets, which published articles containing the details of the alleged fraud. The relators also met with a senator to discuss the suit, though the senator did not speak publically about the fraud until after the seal was partially lifted. The defendant moved to dismiss on the grounds that the relators violated the FCA's seal requirement. The U.S. District Court for the Southern District of Mississippi denied the defendant's motion for dismissal, finding that the *Lujan* factors—(1) harm to the government, (2) the severity of the violations, and (3) evidence of bad faith—favored the relators. The defendant appealed to The U.S. Court of Appeals for the Fifth Circuit, which affirmed the district court's decision to deny dismissal after balancing the *Lujan* factors. The U.S. Supreme Court granted the defendants petition for a writ of certiorari.

The Supreme Court unanimously affirmed the Fifth Circuit's decision to deny the defendants' motion to dismiss, holding that a violation of the FCA's seal requirement does not mandate dismissal. First, the court reasoned that the statute did not include language regarding a remedy for seal violations, and in the absence of remedy guidance, "the sanction for breach is not loss of all later powers to act." Second, the court explained that because the statute contained other provisions that required the dismissal of a relator's action, it could be inferred that if Congress intended to dismiss a *qui tam* suit in response to seal violation, the statute would have said so. Lastly, the court rejected the defendant's argument that a relator's right to bring a *qui tam* action was conditioned on compliance with the seal requirement, explaining that there was no textual indication to support a tie between the seal requirement and relator's right to bring suit.

U.S. ex rel. Evans v. RehabCare Group, Inc. 2016 WL 82334943 (E.D. Mo. Dec. 2, 2016)

Holding: The U.S. District Court for the Eastern District of Missouri granted the relator's motion for voluntary dismissal of her fraudulent therapy services billing claims and denied her motion to temporarily maintain the seal.

The relator brought a *qui tam* suit against the skilled therapy service provider where she was formerly employed and its affiliates, alleging that the defendants submitted claims to the government for services that were medically unnecessary and unreasonable, grossly deficient, not provided at all, and did not meet professional standards of care or the applicable regulations. The government declined to intervene in the relator's suit. The relator then filed a motion to voluntarily dismiss the suit and to maintain the seal on the case filings. The government consented to voluntary dismissal of the complaint, but argued that the case filings should not remain under seal due to the presumption of access to judicial proceedings.

The court granted the relator's motion for voluntary dismissal and denied the relator's motion to maintain the seal on certain case filings. The court explained that relator's argument that she would experience retaliation and difficulty in obtaining employment should her name become public did not distinguish her from employees who bring non-*qui tam* actions against employers, and therefore was not sufficient reason to give special protection to *qui tam* suits or to overcome the strong presumption in favor of public access to judicial records.

Wolff v. Citigroup, Inc., 2016 WL 6945085 (D. Colo. Nov. 2, 2016)

> **Holding: The U.S. District Court for the District of Colorado granted the relator's motion to unseal the government's motion for extension, finding that it did not contain sensitive information.**

The relator brought a *qui tam* suit alleging that a failed Illinois bank violated the False Claims Act by causing the FDIC to pay claims to the bank's creditors that it otherwise would not have paid. Prior to declining to intervene, the government filed a motion for extension of time to decide whether to intervene. After the government declined to intervene, the relator voluntarily dismissed his case, but filed a motion to unseal to the government's motion for an extension. The government opposed the motion, arguing that the motion for an extension contained confidential details regarding investigative strategies.

The court granted the relator's motion to unseal. The court explained that the motion did not contain any sensitive information, instead only "cut and paste" legal standards and a summary of the relator's complaint. However, the court made clear that sensitive statements should remain restricted, even if the remainder of the document is unrestricted.

D. Counterclaims

U.S. ex rel. McIntosh v. Arrow-Med Ambulance, Inc., 2016 WL 6434479 (E.D. Ky. Oct. 27, 2016)

> **Holding:** The U.S. District Court for the Eastern District of Kentucky denied the defendants' motion for leave to file a counterclaim seeking relief against the relator for abuse of civil proceedings, abuse of process, and tortious interference.

In this partially intervened case, the relator brought a *qui tam* action alleging that the defendants submitted false claims for medically unnecessary ambulance transportation in violation of the False Claims Act. The defendants' moved for leave to file a counterclaim proposing to seek relief against the relator for abuse of civil proceedings, abuse of process, and tortious interference with prospective business advantage.

The court denied the defendants' motion for leave to file a counterclaim. The court explained that because the defendant's claims did not present a federal question, did not create diversity of the parties because the claim did not involve any individuals outside of the state of Kentucky, and did not "form part of the same case or controversy" as the relator's action, the counterclaims did not fall within the court's supplemental jurisdiction.

E. Leave to Amend Complaint

U.S. ex rel. D'Agostino v. ev3, Inc., 2016 WL 845 F.3d 1 (1st Cir. Dec. 23, 2016)

> **Holding: The U.S. Court of Appeals for the First Circuit affirmed the district court's decision to deny the realtor's motion to amend his complaint, finding that the complaint failed to state a claim under Rule 12(b)(6).**

The relator brought a *qui tam* action against the medical device manufacturer where he was formerly employed and its subsidiary, alleging that the defendants caused the submission of false reimbursement claims to the government for two of their devices. The relator alleged that the defendants made misrepresentations to induce FDA approval of their product Onyx, encouraged off-label marketing and medically unnecessary use of the Onyx liquid embolic system, failed to provide required training, and concealed manufacturing and design defects. On remand, the U.S. District Court for the District of Massachusetts denied the relator's request to amend his complaint, finding that his claims were precluded by the public disclosure bar, failed to satisfy the particularity requirements of Rule 9(b), and failed to state a claim upon which relief could be granted pursuant to Rule 12(b)(6). The relator appealed to the First Circuit.

The circuit court upheld the district court's decision to deny the relator's motion to amend his complaint. First, the court concluded that the relator did not properly allege a causal link between the defendants' false statements to the FDA and Onyx's approval, or to the subsequent government payment. Additionally, the court noted that the FDA's failure to withdrawal approval despite awareness of the relator's allegations showed that the fraudulent representations were not material to the FDA's decision to approve the drug. Second, the court found that the relator failed to adequately allege that the defendants caused doctors to submit false claims because they did not provide required training, explaining that the FDA-approved label did not contain a requirement that training be given by defendants. Further, the court found that the relator failed to allege with particularity that claims were actually submitted to the government, rejecting the relator's contention that it could be inferred that claims were submitted to the government because many of the defendants' patients were government beneficiaries. Lastly, the court concluded that the relator's complaint failed to provide facts to support his allegations that the relevant products were defective or that any product malfunctions resulted in false claims.

U.S. ex rel. Swoben v. United Healthcare Ins. Co., 848 F.3d 1161 (9th Cir. Dec. 16, 2016)

Holding: The U.S. Court of Appeals for the Ninth Circuit reversed and remanded the district court's decision to deny, on grounds of undue delay, the relator's motion for leave to file a proposed amended complaint, finding that the district court had abused its discretion.

The relator brought a *qui tam* suit against multiple healthcare groups alleging that the defendants falsely certified that the data they submitted to the Center for Medicare & Medicaid Services ("CMS") was "accurate, complete, and truthful." The relator alleged that the defendants conducted biased retrospective reviews of their medical records in which they only identified under-reported diagnosis codes and allowed over-reported diagnosis codes to be erroneously submitted. The U.S. District Court for the Central District of California dismissed the relator's allegations for failure to plead fraud with particularity pursuant to Rule 9(b) and cited undue delay as a basis for denying the relator leave to file a proposed amended complaint. The relator appealed to the Ninth Circuit.

The circuit court reversed and remanded the district court's decision, finding that amendment would not be futile because the relator presented a cognizable legal theory. The court observed that the relator alleged that the defendants took affirmative steps to generate inaccurate data and falsely certified the accuracy of the data reported to CMS in violation of the FCA. The court rejected the defendants' argument that the certifications were not false because the defendants were unaware of unsupported diagnosis codes, and held that the defendants could not shield themselves with retrospective reviews that were designed in bad faith. Furthermore, the court rejected the defendants' argument that their interpretation of CMS guidelines could be considered objectively reasonable, explaining that CMS provided clear guidance regarding the obligation to exercise "due diligence" and ensure "accuracy, completeness, and truthfulness of encounter data." The court further concluded that the relator's complaint adequately alleged the "who, what, when, where, and how of the alleged fraud" regarding some of the defendants, but failed to show a "factual basis" for allegations against other defendants, alleging only a generalized scheme without linking the defendants to the scheme. The court noted that the relator did not need to identify a representative example of false claims for every allegation and could refer to defendants as a collective when multiple defendants engaged in the same conduct. Lastly, the court concluded that the district court abused its discretion in relying on undue delay to justify denying leave to amend, as delay alone could not justify denying leave to amend and the defendants did not demonstrate that they would be prejudiced.

F. Discovery Issues

U.S. ex rel. Cairns v. D.S. Med. L.L.C., 2016 WL 7437919 (E.D. Mo. Dec. 22, 2016)

Holding: The U.S. District Court for the Eastern District of Missouri granted in part the defendant's motion to compel production of the government's reports of interviews from its FCA investigation.

The relator brought a *qui tam* action alleging that a doctor and three affiliates violated the Anti-Kickback Statute, resulting in the submission of tainted claims to the government for spinal surgeries and implant devices in violation of the False Claims Act. Once served with the complaint, the government began parallel civil and criminal investigations and eventually filed its notice of intervention and brought criminal charges against the defendants. The government later dismissed the criminal charges. The U.S. District Court for the Eastern District of Maryland granted the defendants' motion to compel production of the government's privilege log. The government produced a log of interviews, but asserted work product protection over the reports of the contents of these interviews, arguing that they were prepared "in anticipation of possible litigation" and constituted opinion work product. The defendants moved to compel production of the government's reports of interviews.

The court granted in part the defendants' motion to compel production. The court held that though all the reports likely met the "prepared in anticipation of litigation" standard, the government failed to demonstrate that the reports without an attorney's name were opinion work product. With respect to the pre-intervention interviews, the court found that the defendants demonstrated substantial need for the reports, explaining that conducting depositions would be unsatisfactory due to the passage of time and consequent memory lapse since the interviews. However, the court found that the defendants did not demonstrate substantial need for reports of post-intervention interviews, as depositions would produce the same relevant information. Finally, the court concluded it was unclear whether the remaining reports with associated attorney names were fact or opinion work product, and therefore the court would conduct an *in camera* review to determine whether or not the reports were protected.

G. Default Judgment

U.S. ex rel. Washington v. Morad, 2016 WL 7187932 (E.D. La. Dec. 12, 2016)

Holding: The U.S. District Court for the Eastern District of Louisiana granted the relator's motion for default judgment on relator's allegations that the defendant billed for services not provided and falsely certified patient statuses.

The relator brought a *qui tam* suit against multiple individuals and health care service companies, alleging that the defendants conspired to defraud the government by submitting claims for payment to the government for services that were not provided in violation of the False Claims Act. All defendants were served with process, but failed to respond to the summons and complaint, and did not request additional time to respond. The relator moved for default judgment and sought damages.

The court granted the relator's motion for default judgment, holding that the relator's well-pleaded factual allegations were deemed admitted due to the defendants' failure to appear, and that those allegations established a *prima facie* FCA claim. The court ordered the relator to submit "summary-judgment type" evidence that would allow the court to calculate the amount of damages.

H.   Relator's Share

U.S. ex rel. Wittenberg v. Pub. Util. Dist. No. 1 of Skamania Cty., 2016 WL 6518438 (D. Or. Nov. 1, 2016)

Holding: The U.S. District Court for the District of Oregon granted the relator's motion for a relator's share in part, finding that the information he contributed to the government's investigation was valuable but not indispensable to the ultimate settlement of the case.

The relator brought a *qui tam* action against a municipal electricity corporation where he was formerly employed as general manager, alleging that the defendant reported higher pole line miles in order to obtain a larger rural utility provider discount from the government, in violation of the False Claims Act. Prior to filing suit and not as part of his employment, the relator mapped the defendant's pole line miles and discovered that the miles reported were inaccurate, and after filing suit shared his calculations with the government. Throughout the case, the relator continued to be helpful and engaged. However, the government contracted a third-party firm to calculate pole line miles, and the firm produced a different number different than the relator's original calculation. The third-party's calculation was used in the settlement, and the relator's share remained undetermined. The relator moved to receive an award of 24%, while the government proposes an award of 17%.

The court granted the relator's motion in part, finding that 20% was an appropriate award. The court explained that though the government had no prior knowledge of relator's information, the relator deserved an award closer to the statutory minimum than statutory maximum because he did not develop all relevant facts to complete accuracy, his information was only somewhat significant, and his contribution was not vital. The court noted that an award of 20% captured the relevant contributions of the relator and the third party, as well as the government's use of both sources of information.

I. Affirmative Defenses

U.S. ex rel. Feaster v. Dopps Chiropractic Clinic, LLC, 2016 WL 6462041, (D. Kan. Nov. 1, 2016)

Holding: The U.S. District Court for the District of Kansas granted the relator's motion to strike fourteen of the defendants' and twenty defenses and affirmative defenses in part.

The relator brought a *qui tam* suit against the chiropractic clinic where he was formerly employed and its owner, alleging that the defendants billed Medicare for unperformed, uncovered, unnecessary, or undocumented services in violation of the False Claims Act. The defendant filed an Answer to the relator's second amended complaint, which contained twenty defenses and affirmative defenses. The relator moved to strike, or in the alternative order defendant to clarify, fourteen of defendants' twenty defenses.

The court granted the relator's motion in part, striking defendants' second, third, and eighth defenses and allowing defendant to amend its fifth and thirteenth defense. The court determined that defendants' second and third defenses, in which they argued that the relator failed to allege an FCA claim, were no longer valid because the court already determined through a motion to dismiss that the realtor sufficiently stated a claim. Further, the court found that the defendants' eighth defense, in which they argued that the relator lacked standing, failed as a matter of law. However, the court refused to strike the defendants' unclean hands defenses and original source defense. Further, the court allowed the defendants' damages defense, as well as their defense arguing that the defendants were not proper parties. The court also declined to strike the defendants' defense arguing that the defendants' made a good faith effort to comply with Title IV.

J.   Settlement Agreements

U.S. ex rel. Doghramji v. Cmty. Health Sys., Inc., 2016 WL 6872051 (6th Cir. Nov. 22, 2016)

> **Holding: The U.S. Court of Appeals for the Sixth Circuit reversed and remanded the district court's adoption of the relator's interpretation of the settlement agreement.**

In this intervened case, seven relators brought seven different *qui tam* suits against a hospital services provider, all alleging that the defendant violated the False Claims Act by admitting patients for medically-unnecessary emergency room visits. The government settled all of the cases and the relators entered into a sharing agreement for the purposes of relator's share and the award of attorney's fees and costs. The defendant challenged the ability of some of the relators to collect fees and costs, citing the first-to-file bar. The U.S. District Court for the Middle District of Tennessee found that the defendant waived the right to make this argument because the contract language only allowed for the defendant to challenge the amount of fees and costs, not the ability to recover them at all. The defendant appealed to the Sixth Circuit.

The circuit court reversed and remanded the district court's order. The circuit court found that both the relator and defendant argued reasonable interpretations of the settlement agreement's language. Because the agreement was subject to two reasonable interpretations, the court concluded that the provision was ambiguous and remanded to the district court to consider extrinsic evidence to determine the parties' original understanding of the agreement.

K. Primary Jurisdiction of Agency

U.S. v. Savannah River Nuclear Sol., LLC, 2016 WL 7104823 (D. S.C. Dec. 6, 2016)

> **Holding: The U.S. District Court for the District of South Carolina denied the defendants' motion to dismiss and stayed case proceedings until the Civilian Board of Contract Appeals provided an advisory opinion on relevant contract requirements with which the defendants' allegedly falsely certified compliance.**

The government brought a suit under the False Claims Act alleging that the defendants overbilled the government under their contracts to provide management and operations support for a government facility that processed and stored nuclear material. The government alleged that the contracts prohibited the defendants from billing for certain costs and expenses, and that the defendants billed for these expenses anyway while falsely certifying that they had complied with the contract terms. The defendants moved to dismiss the government's claims for failure to plead fraud with particularity under Rule 9(b) and for failure to state a claim upon under Rule 12(b)(6).

The court denied the defendants' motion to dismiss, but stayed case proceedings until the Civilian Board of Contract Appeals ("CBCA") issued an advisory opinion. The court concluded that the government's claims satisfied Rule 9(b)'s particularity requirements. The court observed that the complaint specified annual costs included in claims, the amount, invoice numbers, and dates of separate allegedly false invoices. However, the court indicated that the falsity and reasonableness of the defendants' interpretation of the contract terms were best decided after obtaining an advisory opinion from the CBCA, a government contract advisory board. Additionally, the court rejected the defendants' "government knowledge" argument, noting that the complaint contained no evidence to demonstrate that the government continued to approve claims, "willingly acquiesced," or that the defendants thought costs were allowable *"because* the [government] continued to pay." Lastly, the court explained that the government sufficiently alleged materiality by demonstrating that a causal relationship existed between defendants' annual certifications and payment.

L.   Statistical Sampling

U.S. ex rel. Tessler v. City of New York, 2016 WL 7335654 (S.D.N.Y. Dec. 16, 2016)

> **Holding: The U.S. District Court for the Southern District of New York granted the defendant's motion to dismiss the relator's allegations that the defendant submitted false claims under federally-funded aid programs for failure to plead fraud with particularity under Rule 9(b) and failure to state a claim under Rule 12(b)(6).**

The relator brought a *qui tam* suit against his former employer, the City of New York, alleging that the defendant violated the False Claims Act in its administration of its Supplemental Nutrition Assistance Program ("SNAP"), Temporary Assistance for Needy Families ("TANF"), and Medicare Savings Program. Specifically, the relator alleged that the defendant failed to attempt to correct overpayments distributed through SNAP and TANF during recipients' eligibility hearings and failed to meet its obligation to review beneficiaries' eligibility for the Medicare Savings Program. The defendant moved to dismiss the relator's claims for failure to plead fraud with particularity under Rule 9(b) and failure to state a claim under Rule 12(b)(6).

The court granted the defendant's motion to dismiss. The court found that the relator's SNAP and TANF claims failed to meet the requirements of Rule 9(b), explaining that the relator failed to identify a specific false claim submitted to the government as a result of the defendant's alleged improper conduct. The court found that relator's statistical evidence was not sufficient to bolster his claims in order to satisfy Rule 9(b). Additionally, the court explained that the relator failed to demonstrate an adequate basis for his knowledge because the allegedly fraudulent conduct occurred in connection with activities outside the scope of his employment and during a time period before he was employed with the defendant. With respect to the relator's Medicare Savings Program allegations, the court concluded that the relator failed to identify a specific law that the defendants violated.

U.S. ex rel. Hagerty v. Cyberonics, 844 F.3d 26 (1st Cir. Dec. 16, 2016)

> **Holding: The U.S. Court of Appeals for the First Circuit affirmed the district court's decision to dismiss the relator's off-label marketing claims for failure to plead fraud with particularity under Rule 9(b).**

The relator brought a *qui tam* suit against the medical device manufacturer where he was formerly employed, alleging that the defendant caused patients and medical providers to submit false claims to the government for unnecessary replacement of medical device batteries in violation of the False Claims Act. The relator further alleged that the defendant incentivized sales staff to use fraudulent sales tactics by rewarding achievement of aggressive sales quotas and punishing staff for failure to meet those goals. The U.S. District Court for the District of Massachusetts granted the defendant's motion to dismiss the relator's allegations for failure to plead fraud with particularity under Rule 9(b) and denied the relator's motion for leave to amend his complaint. The relator appealed to the First Circuit.

The circuit court upheld the district court's decision to dismiss the relator's complaint and deny the relator leave to amend his complaint. The court held that the relator's complaint failed to allege with requisite particularity that medical providers actually submitted claims to the government for unnecessary battery replacements or that any patients that received the replacements were covered by government healthcare programs. Moreover, the court explained that the relator's use of statistical sampling to support his allegation that 10,000 false claims were submitted to the government could not satisfy the particularity requirements of Rule 9(b), as his statements did not link the defendant's revenue to the alleged fraudulent procedures and were "too broad" to provide any basis for his claims. Additionally, the court concluded that the court did not abuse its discretion in denying the relator leave to amend his complaint, explaining that the relator did not provide justification for the significant delay in moving to amend.

Judgments &
Settlements

OCTOBER 1, 2016–DECEMBER 31, 2016

Bay Sleep Clinic and Related Entities (N.D. Cal. Dec. 28, 2016)

Bay Sleep Clinic, and its related businesses, Qualium Corporation and Amerimed Corporation, and their owners and operators Anooshiravan Mostowfipour and Tara Nadar will pay $2.6 million to resolve allegations that they violated the False Claims Act by billing Medicare for diagnostic sleep tests and devices that violated Medicare rules and regulations. Specifically, the government alleges that Bay Sleep Clinic and the related entities submitted claims for services performed by technicians who lacked necessary certification, falsified documents to appear as if services were performed in Medicare approved locations, and improperly shared a location with a durable medical equipment provider. In addition to the settlement, Bay Sleep Clinic voluntarily terminated their two existing Medicare enrollments and agreed to refrain from enrolling any providers for three years. TAFEF members Anne Hayes Hartman and Jessica Moore of Constantine Cannon represented the relator in this case.

United Shore Financial Services LLC (E.D. Mich. And W.D. Wis. Dec. 28, 2016)

United Shore Financial Services LLC ("USFS") agreed to pay $48 million to settle allegations that it knowingly originated and underwrote mortgage loans insured under the U.S. Department of Housing and Urban Development's Federal Housing Administration ("FHA") that were not qualified under FHA standards. Additionally, the government contends that USFS failed to comply with required quality control standards and inappropriately pressured underwriters to approve unqualified FHA mortgages. The settlement resolves allegations of USFS misconduct between January 1, 2006 and December 31, 2011

Advanced C4 Solutions, Inc. (D. Md. Dec. 28, 2016)

Advanced C4 Solutions, Inc., a Florida-based defense contractor, will pay $4.535 million to resolve allegations under the False Claims Act that it submitted inflated invoices to the government for work performed at Joint Base Andrews. Allegedly, Advanced C4 Solutions certified that it was a certified small business under the Small Business Act when it did not actually qualify as a small business. Additionally, Advanced C4 Solutions allegedly submitted invoices from its subcontractor, Superior Communication Solutions, Inc. ("SCSI") despite knowing that SCSI was charging for labor hours not actually performed and job classification rates for personnel without the required credentials. The settlement also resolves allegations against the project's manager, Andrew Bennet, who was responsible for submitting the SCSI's invoices to the government.

Total Call Mobile, LLC (S.D.N.Y. Dec. 22, 2016)

Total Call Mobile, LLC ("Total Call") agreed to pay $30 million to resolve False Claims Act allegations that it knowingly defrauded the Lifeline Program, a federal government mobile phone subsidy program that offers discounted mobile phone services to low-income customers. The government alleged that Total Call knowingly submitted reimbursement claims for customers who did not meet the Lifeline Program's eligibility requirements and that Total Call falsely certified compliance with the FCC that it was abiding by the Lifeline Program's requirements. Specifically, Total Call allegedly used in-person sales tactics to gain customers so that Total Call employees could enter customer demographics themselves, and therefore engage in fraudulent enrollment methods including using the same eligibility proof on multiple customers, tamper with identification documentation, purposefully alter customer input for the benefit of Total Call, and submit entirely false information. Moreover, the government alleged that Total Call did not implement any proper security, procedures, or fraud preventative reviews of enrollments and continued to approve their enrollments despite knowledge of misconduct. As part of the settlement, Total Call accepted responsibility for the conduct alleged in the complaint and agreed to not participate in the Lifeline Program. TAFEF member Johnathan Willens of Willens & Scarvalon represented the relator in this settlement.

SandRidge Energy Inc. (Dec. 20, 2016)

SandRidge Energy Inc., an Oklahoma-based oil and gas company, agreed to pay a $1.4 million penalty to settle charges with the SEC that it used employee separation agreements that violated SEC regulations and also terminated an employee in retaliation for raising concerns regarding how the company calculated its reserves. The SEC contends that SandRidge Energy Inc. violated SEC employee separation agreement regulations by prohibiting outgoing employees from participating in government investigations or disclosing information to the government that could potentially harm the company.

Wallace Construction and Rosciti Construction (D.R.I. Dec. 19, 2016)

Two Rhode Island construction companies, Wallace Construction ("Wallace") and Rosciti Construction ("Rosciti"), will pay $1 million to resolve allegations under the False Claims Act that they submitted reimbursement requests or caused the submission of reimbursement requests for work completed on a contract designated for "disadvantaged businesses enterprises" ("DBE") when in fact they did not qualify as a DBE. Specifically, the government contends that Rosciti subcontracted Wallace on an Environmental Protection Agency ("EPA"), Department of Education, and Department of Transportation funded contract for roadways, water systems, and parking improvements that contained specific requirements that the project's subcontractors include minority-owned, women-owned, or small businesses, even though Wallace was not a DBE and lacked the capacity to perform the necessary work on the projects. In addition to the settlement, Rosciti and Wallace entered administrative agreements with the EPA to resolve further potential claims and appointed internal compliance officers and a third-party external monitor to prevent future misconduct.

Forest Laboratories LLC (E.D. Wis Dec. 15, 2016)

Forest Laboratories LLC and its subsidiary Forest Pharmaceuticals, Inc. agreed to pay $38 million to settle allegations that it violated the Anti-Kickback Statute ("AKS") by inducing physicians to prescribe Bystolic, Savella, or Namenda by paying kickbacks to physicians in the form of payments and meals in connection with speaker programs about the respective drugs. The government alleged that Forest Laboratories' payments and meals violated the AKS because they were provided even if the programs were cancelled, if no licensed health professionals were present, or if meal programs exceeded Forest Laboratories' internal budget. The *qui tam* suit was brought by a former employee who will receive a $7.8 million reward as part of the settlement.

Elite Lab Services LLC (E.D. Tex. Dec. 14, 2016)

Elite Lab Services LLC agreed to pay $3.75 million to resolve allegations that it violated the False Claims Act by inflating mileage claims. In the settlement, Elite Lab Services LLC and its husband-and-wife owners admitted that they billed Medicare for tens of thousands of miles that were never actually driven. The *qui tam* suit was brought by a former employee who contends that before resigning her employment she raised concerns about Elite Lab Services LLC inflated mileage. The relator will receive a 21% share as a part of the settlement.

Lynn Madsen (D. Vt. Dec. 14, 2016)

Lynn Madsen, a Vermont pain management doctor, agreed to pay $76,000 to resolve allegations that she violated the False Claims Act by knowingly presenting or causing to be presented false claims to Medicare or Medicaid for services that were not medically reasonable or necessary. Allegedly, Madsen administered trigger point injections devoid of any therapeutic agent, most often containing only saline or saline-based injectates. According to the complaint, Madsen submitted hundreds of claims that violated Medicare and Medicaid laws regulations, and program limitations.

Atlanta Workforce Development Agency's (N.D. Ga. Dec. 13, 2016)

The Atlanta Workforce Development Agency's ("AWDA") agreed to pay $1.86 million to resolve allegations under the False Claims Act that it falsely certified that it distributed grant money from the Department of Education to employers administering "federal on-the-job training" to unemployed job seekers. Instead, the AWDA allegedly distributed the grant money to employers who used it to train already existing employees, in violation of grant stipulations and federal regulations. The government also settled allegations against AWDA in connection with its former budget analyst and nightclub owner, Kevin Edward, who pleaded guilty to one count of stealing federal funds by submitting forged and fraudulent wage reimbursements for employees who never actually worked for his companies or instead of receiving skills training, completed "odd-jobs" such as cleaning or yard work. Over three years, Edwards received approximately $649,000 in grant money from the AWDA.

Bristol-Myers Squibb (D. Del. Dec. 8, 2016)

Bristol-Myers Squibb will pay $19.5 million to 42 states in order to settle allegations that it engaged in off-label marketing of the anti-psychotic drug, Abilify. Allegedly, Bristol-Myers Squibb marketed Abilify to children and elderly patients presenting symptoms of dementia or Alzheimer's disease even though Abilify was never approved for that use and received a warning against use on elderly patients with dementia or Alzheimer's. Furthermore, the government contended that Bristol-Myers Squibb minimized safety risks and overstated findings of scientific studies, mirroring the allegations of Bristol-Myers Squibb's previous $515 million settlement in 2007. Delaware's Consumer Protection Fund will receive $389,677 of the settlement while $19.5 million will be distributed to the remainder of the States and the District of Columbia.

Southeast Orthopedic Specialists (M.D. Fla. Dec. 7, 2016)

Southeast Orthopedic Specialists will pay $4.488 million to settle allegations that they violated the False Claims Act by billing for medically unnecessary and unreasonable services. The government contends that Southeast Orthopedic Specialists sought reimbursement for services that did not meet required "meaningful use" standards, knowingly billed for services that failed to meet government requirements, upcoded services, and administered services for the sole purpose of obtaining greater funds. Allegedly, Southeast Orthopedic Specialists fraudulent conduct resulted in millions of dollars of questionable claims.

South Miami Hospital (S.D. Fla. Dec. 7, 2016)

South Miami Hospital, a not-for-profit regional hospital, agreed to pay $12 million to settle allegations that it violated the False Claims Act by submitting claims to government insurance programs for medically unnecessary services and studies. Specifically, South Miami Hospital allegedly requested payment for heart-procedures, cardiac catheterizations, and electrophysiology studies and procedures. This suit was brought by a board-certified vascular surgeon and a medical doctor practicing at South Miami Hospital.

Summit Medical Group (D. N.J. Dec. 7, 2016)

Summit Medical Group agreed to pay $9 million to resolve allegations under the False Claims Act that it admitted Medicare patients under "inpatient status," even though the patients actually qualified under the less expensive "observational status," or should not have been admitted at all. Additionally, Summit Medical Group allegedly unnecessarily kept patients in hospitals for three day stays or longer in order to receive greater Medicare benefits at Skilled Nursing Facilities when patients were discharged. TAFEF member Timothy McInnis of McInnis Law represented the relators, two healthcare professionals, in this settlement.

Lifepoint Dental Group, LLC (N.D. Iowa Dec. 7, 2016)

Lifepoint Dental Group, LLC and its owners Aaron Blass, Angelina Blass, Mindy Richtsmeir, and Brad Richtsmeier will pay more than $300,000 to resolve allegations that they violated the False Claims Act by submitting claims for services that were medically unnecessary or did not occur at all. The settlement covered alleged misconduct between April 1, 2015 and October 1, 2015. The suit was brought by two *qui tam* relators who were both formerly employed with Lifepoint Dental Group, LLC.

Robert S. Luce (E.D. Ill. Dec. 1, 2016)

A federal judge found Robert S. Luce liable for $3,452,499 for certifying loans to the Department of Housing and Urban Development and the Federal Housing Administration under false verification forms. Luce personally signed 237 defaulted mortgage loans while operating his mortgage company, MDR Mortgage Corporation. In addition to the settlement, he consented to a five-month suspension of his law license.

Allied Home Mortgage Capital Corporation (S.D. Tex. Nov. 30, 2016)

A jury found Allied Home Mortgage Capital Corporation ("Allied Capital") liable for $92,982,775 million based on its fraudulent misconduct associated with falsely certifying loans to the Federal Housing Administration (FHA). Specifically, Allied

Capital knowingly certified loans that were ineligible for FHA mortgage insurance and misrepresented to FHA that the loans were certified with due diligence. The jury found that Allied Capital recklessly underwrote and certified at least 1,192 loans for FHA insurance, resulting in an $85,615,643 loss. Separately, Allied Capital will be subject to a statutory penalty under FIRREA.

MedNet, Inc. (D.N.J. Nov. 29, 2016)

MedNet, Inc. ("MedNet'), presently a subsidiary of BioTelemetry, Inc., will pay $1.35 million to settle allegations that they violated the Anti-Kickback Statute (AKS) and False Claims Act by creating agreements that improperly induced its healthcare provider customers to use MedNet's cardiac monitoring services. Specifically, MedNet's improper agreements enabled providers to directly bill Medicare for MedNet's services which allowed them to retain Medicare payments, in excess of MetNet's fees. TAFEF members Suzanne Durrell and Robert Thomas, Jr. of Whistleblower Law Collaborative represented the relator in this settlement.

Leatha Henderson (E.D. Cal. Nov. 28, 2016)

Leatha Henderson, a Sacramento Landlord, will pay $75,000 to resolve allegations that she violated the False Claims Act by submitting false claims to the government while participating in The Housing Choice Voucher Program, a federal housing subsidy program commonly known as "Section 8." Specifically, Henderson allegedly falsely certified compliance with the program's restriction to not charge tenants more than 32-38% of the total rent. The whistleblower will receive a $13,500 reward as part of the settlement.

Bechtel National and AECOM (E.D. Wash. Nov. 23, 2016)

Bechtel National and its primary subcontractor, AECOM, agreed to pay $125 million to settle allegations under the False Claims Act that it charged the Department of Energy for materials and work that failed to comply with required quality control standards for nuclear facilities. Furthermore, Bechtel and its subcontractor allegedly violated the Byrd Amendment by misusing federal funds to engage in a political campaign. The government contends that Bechtel spent federal funds supporting a campaign that intended to lobby Congress for more funds to complete work on Bechtel's nuclear reservation and also to downplay the significance of nuclear safety regulations. All whistleblowers in this settlement were key, former managers at Bechtel National.

Dr. Anthony Clavo (N.D. Ga. Nov. 23, 2016)

Dr. Anthony Clavo, a pain management physician will pay $430,000 to the entry of a consent judgment that he violated the False Claims Act by billing Medicare, Medicaid, and TRICARE for services that were either medically unnecessary or were administered without sufficient information to conclude the medical service was necessary. The settlement covers Dr. Clavo's alleged misconduct between January 1, 2014 and June 22, 2015. The *qui tam* suit was brought by two of Dr. Clavo's former employees.

ManTech International (E.D. Va. Nov. 22, 2016)

A jury found ManTech International ("ManTech"), a defense contractor, liable for a total of $800,000 in compensatory damages plus respective back pay due to ManTech's retaliatory termination of two relator executives. The relator executives, Kevin Cody and his wife Muge Cody, were terminated after reporting billing fraud on a US government contract. The jury returned a verdict of $500,000 plus $857,846 in back pay and $300,000 plus $496,370 in backpay to Kevin Cody and Muge Cody, respectively. TAFEF members Scott Oswald and Tom Harrington of The Employment Law Group represented the relators in this matter.

Mousetrap Pediatrics PC (D. Vt. Nov. 18, 2016)

Mousetrap Pediatrics PC will pay $6,706,918.65 to settle allegations that it violated the False Claims Act by improperly coding for medical services. Specifically, Mousetrap Pediatrics allegedly billed the government for services provided during regular service hours as services provided during extended office hours. It was determined that the improper billing resulted from a change in practices and was not intentional. Mousetrap Pediatrics will reimburse Medicaid $51,553.65 in addition to a $15,000 fine and will pay the State of Vermont $6,655,365.

Zwanger & Pesiri Radiology Group LLP (E.D.N.Y. Nov. 16, 2016)

Zwanger & Pesiri Radiology Group LLP ("Zwanger & Pesiri"), a Long Island radiology company, pleaded guilty to two counts of health care fraud and agreed to pay over $8.1 million to resolve its civil liability under the False Claims Act. Zwanger & Pesiri was guilty of illegally performing and billing for medical services that were never actually ordered and automatically bundling medical tests. Zwanger & Pesiri's civil settlement also addresses allegations that Zwanger & Pesiri billed Medicare and Medicaid for procedures that were performed without the required supervision of credentialed physicians or were performed at locations not authorized by the federal insurance programs. As a part of the settlement, Zwanger & Pesiri agreed to enter a Corporate Integrity Agreement.

Niurka Fernandez and Robert Alverez (S.D. Fla. Nov. 8, 2016)

Niurka Fernandez and Robert Alverez, mother and son, will pay $9.5 million and $1.5 million in restitution and serve 120 and 30 months in prison respectively for pleading guilty to co-owning and operating pharmacies for the sole purpose of submitting false and fraudulent claims to Medicare Part D, in violation of the False Claims Act. Specifically, Fernandez organized and led the scheme to pay Medicare beneficiaries and patient recruiters for medically unnecessary prescriptions, and further paid kickbacks to pharmacies to conceal her fraudulent scheme. Alverez pleaded guilty to participating in the conspiracy by, among other actions, writing checks to money launderers to obtain kickbacks. In total, Medicare paid at least $9.5 million in overpayments as a result of Fernandez and Alverez misconduct.

Dan Horsky (E.D. Va. Nov. 7, 2016)

Dan Horksy, a former professor of business administration in New York pleaded guilty to conspiring to defraud the government and submitted false expatriation statements to the IRS, paying a $100 million penalty fee. Specifically, Horsky invested in many offshore banks and created a nominee entity entitled "Horsky Holdings" in order to conceal his offshore financial transitions and accounts from the government. Horsky will face a statutory maximum of five years in prison in addition to a period of supervised release.

Network Services Solutions (Nov. 8, 2016)

Network Services Solutions and its CEO, will pay the FCC a $21 million dollar fine for defrauding and bribing a Rural Health Care Program in order to influence contract awards. The FCC charged Network Services Solutions with violating competitive bidding rules, using forged and false documents to obtain funding, and violating the federal wire fraud statute. In addition to the penalty payments, the FCC required the company to refund the $3.5 million improper payments Network Services Solutions received.

Biocompatibles (W.D.Tex. Nov. 7, 2016)

Biocompatibles, a medical device manufacturer and subsidiary of BTG PLC pleaded guilty to charges of falsely marketing an embolic device and will pay $36 million to resolve both civil and criminal liability. Specifically, Biocompatibles told the FDA that "under no circumstance" could it market its approved medical device for drug delivery purposes because clinical studies did not demonstrate adequate evidence of therapeutic benefit, however Biocompatibles later marketed the device for drug delivery. Biocompatibles specifically marketed within the chemoembolization market by advising healthcare providers that the device was "better" for certain types of cancer. A high ranking marketing professional brought the *qui tam* suit was brought and significantly aided the investigation by wearing a wire to record conversations. The relator will receive a 21.5% share in the settlement. The relator was represented by TAFEF members Paul Lawrence of Water & Kraus.

Air Industries Corporation (C.D. Cal. Nov. 4, 2016)

Air Industries Corporation ("AIC"), an aerospace company, will pay $2.7 million to resolve allegations that it violated the False Claims Act by falsely certifying that it performed required inspections on aerospace parts for military aircrafts, space crafts, and missiles. The *qui tam* suit was brought by an employee of AIC who will receive a $621,000 award as part of the settlement. The relator was represented by TAFEF members David Caputo and David William of Kline & Specter, PC and Joseph Trautwein of Joseph Trautwein & Associates.

Ormat Technologies, Inc. (D. Nev. Nov. 1, 2016)

Ormat Technologies, Inc. agreed to pay $5.5 million to resolve allegations under the False Claims Act that they received millions of dollars in clean energy grants that they were not entitled to by misleading the government on the dates projects were in service, the amount of power produced, their long term viability, and the purpose of site expansion projects. Allegedly, Ormat Technologies fraudulently reported the amount of energy the plant only generated in order to delay termination of their project. Additionally, the relators alleged that Ormat Technologies began operated a geothermal plant before regulators approved their qualifications or ability to sell power. TAFEF members John Yanchunis, James D. Young, and Patrik Barthle, II, of Morgan & Morgan, P.A.; Laura S. Dunning, Peter Mougey, and Christopher Gus Paulos, of Levin Papantonio, Thomas, Mitchell, Rafferty and Proctor; and Don Springmeyer, of Wolf, Rifkin, Shapiro, Schulman and Rabkin, LLP all contributed to the settlement.

Life Care Centers (E.D. Tenn. Oct. 24, 2016)

Life Care Centers agreed to pay $145 million to settle allegations that its corporate-wide policies caused the submission of claims to government programs that were not reasonable or necessary, in violation of the False Claims Act. Allegedly, Life Care Centers employed internal policies that ensured the largest number of patients would qualify for the most expensive category of skilled therapy and nursing services, regardless of whether the patients actually needed the highest level of services. The settlement also addresses allegations that Life Care Centers kept rehabilitation patients longer than medically necessary in order to obtain larger reimbursements from government insurance programs. As a part of the settlement, Life Care Centers will enter into a Corporate Integrity Agreement to ensure accurate assessment of medical necessity and appropriateness. TAFEF members Mark Simpson and Michael Sullivan represented the relator in this settlement.

Hudson Valley Associates, RLLP (S.D.N.Y. Oct. 21, 2016)

Hudson Valley Associates, RLLP ("HVA") agreed to pay $5.31 million to resolve allegations that it violated the False Claims Act by fraudulently billing Medicare for payments that resulted from unlawfully waived co-payments. HVA also allegedly systematically submitted false claims for services that it did not actual provide or were not permitted. HVA admitted, acknowledged, and accepted responsibility for its fraudulent conduct as a part of the settlement.

K3 Learning, Inc. (Oct. 21, 2016)

K3 Learning, Inc. and its President Michael Koffler will pay over $4.3 million to resolve allegations that its special education preschool, Sunshine Development School, over charged the State of New York for services and engaged in a scheme to under-report millions in personal and corporate income tax, in violation of the False Claims Act. Additionally, K3 Learning, Inc. created a leasing arrangement in which Koffler's contractor rented the building and also rented a pass-through building in order to lease the preschool at substantial markup. Moreover, Koffler allegedly engaged in kick-back schemes from 2006 to 2010.

Omnicare, Inc. (W.D. Va. Oct., 17 2016)

Omnicare, Inc., the largest nursing home pharmacy in the United States, agreed to pay $28.125 million to settle allegations that violated the False Claims Act and Anti-Kickback Statute by soliciting and receiving kickbacks from Abbott Labs, a healthcare manufacturer, in exchange for promoting and prescribing an anti-epileptic drug for nursing home residents. Specifically, the relator contends that Omnicare disguised the kickbacks by describing them as "grant" or "educational" funds. Abbott Labs' liability was settled in a previous settlement. TAFEF member-firm Simmer Law Group represented the relator in this settlement.

Five Rochester-area Contractors (October 14, 2016)

Five Rochester, New York contractors will pay $825,000 fine to settle allegations that they violated the False Claims Act while working on a $1.2 billion dollar government contract, the largest public contract in the city's history. Allegedly, the companies falsely claimed to meet the minority-and-women-owned business standards required to win the government contract. The companies also allegedly engaged in "labor pass-through" in which they created the appearance of hiring minority-owned businesses to perform labor, but only ran paperwork through it. The five companies are Concord Electric Company, Michael Ferraulio Plumbing & Heating, Manning Squires Henning Co. Inc., Hewit Young Electric LLC, Mark Cerrone, Inc. and will pay $350,000; $200,000; $160,000; $90,000; and $25,000 respectively.

Gateway, Inc. (Oct. 11, 2016)

After 13 years of litigation, Gateway, Inc. and its subsidiary Cowabunga Enterprises, will settle allegations that it violated the False Claims Act by failing to collect and remit Illinois use tax on its internet sales in a settlement of $6.27 million. Allegedly, Gateway and Cowabunga sold untaxed merchandise over the internet to Illinois customers despite having representatives or agents in Illinois. TAFEF members Stephen Diamond and Matthew Burns of Stephen Diamond, PC represented the relator in this settlement.

Mylan (D. Mass. Oct. 7, 2016)

Mylan will pay $456 million to settle allegations that it violated the False Claims Act by overcharging Medicaid and Medicare by knowingly misclassifying the Epipen as a generic drug, causing government programs to pay more in rebates than they otherwise would have paid. Allegedly, Mylan and previous drug makers had been misclassifying the Epipen since at least 1997, allegedly totaling nearly $1.3 billion in payments. As a part of the settlement, Mylan will enter a Corporate Integrity Agreement.

Whittier Health Network, Inc. (D. Mass. Oct. 13, 2016)

Whittier Health Network, a Massachusetts-based nursing home operator, agreed to pay $2.5 million to settle False Claims Act allegations that it submitted claims to Medicare for therapy, when in fact therapists were only providing initial evaluations. Allegedly, Whittier Health Network, Inc. therapists also violated Medicare rules by rounding up the actual minutes of provided therapy. The relator who brought the *qui tam* suit will receive a 30% relator share, or $750,000, as part of the settlement. The relator was represented by TAFEF member Louise Herman of the Law Offices of Louise Herman.

Burlington Labs Inc. and Burlington Labs LLC (D. Vt. Oct. 11, 2016)

Burlington Labs Inc. and Burlington Labs LLC ("Burlington Labs") agreed to pay $6.75 million to settle allegations that it submitted false claims or received overpayments from the Vermont Medicaid Program, in violation of the False Claims Act. Specifically, Burlington Labs allegedly varied how they charged Medicare for specific-drug screening and confirmatory tests based on the number of drugs tested, in violation of Medicare program rules. In conjunction with their settlement, Burlington Labs entered into a Corporate Integrity Agreement which includes independent review of sample claims for up to five years.

Novartis Pharmaceuticals Corporation (E.D. Penn. Oct. 6, 2016)

Novartis Pharmaceuticals Corporation ("Novartis") agreed to pay $35 million to set-tle allegations under the False Claims Act that it engaged in off-label marketing of its eczema cream, Elidel. The relator alleges that the FDA explicitly did not approve us-ing the cream on infants, as it could cause skin cancer and non-Hodgkin's lymphoma, yet Novartis instructed its sales representatives to tell doctors it was safe for infants, capitalizing on the concept of "steroid-phobia," a Novartis term used to boost prescrib-ers. The relator also alleged that Novartis engaged in a kickback scheme in which it paid doctors to attend expensive dinners and conferences where off-label uses of Elidel were promoted. TAFEF members Jennifer Verkamp, Frederick Morgan, and Maxwell Smith of Morgan Verkamp represented the relator in this settlement.

Armor Correctional Health Services (Oct. 5, 2016)

Armor Correctional Health Services ("Armor"), a jail health services company respon-sible for inmate medical services in Nassau County of New York, will pay $350,000 to resolve allegations that it violated the False Claims Act by failing to properly perform or seriously underperforming its contractual obligations. Specifically, Armor allegedly failed to provide timely reports of key health statistics. As part of the settlement, Ar-mor agreed not to bid on any contracts in Nassau County and New York State for three years. The New York Office of the Attorney General will retain $100,000 of the settlement, while the affected New York County will receive $250,000.

Yavapai Regional Medical Center (D. Ariz. Oct. 4, 2016)

Yavapai Regional Medical Center, a non-for-profit community health system, will pay $5.85 million to resolve claims that it violated the False Claims Act by misreporting the amount of hours its employees worked in its annual cost reports. Yavapai Regional Medical Center's improper reporting caused Yavapai Regional Medical Center to re-ceive more money from Medicare than they otherwise would have received, as their improper reporting raised Medicare's wage index, thus skewing Medicare's calcula-tions. The settlement resolves alleged conduct between 2006 and 2009. The relator will receive a $1.17 million share of the settlement.

Primary Residential Mortgage Inc. and Security National Mortgage Company (D. Colo. Oct. 4, 2016)

Primary Residential Mortgage Inc. (PRMI) and Security National Mortgage Com-pany (SNMC), both headquartered in Utah, agreed to pay $5 million and $4.25 mil-lion respectively to settle allegations under the False Claims Act that they knowingly originated and underwrote loans insured by the Department of Housing and Urban

Development (HUD) that did not meet the HUD's loan requirements. Among multiple statements of fact, both companies admitted in the settlement that they endorsed loans that did not meet HUD's requirements.

Three Orthopedic Clinics (E.D. Cal. Oct. 3, 2016)

Orthopedic Associates of Northern California, San Bernardino, Medical Orthopedic Group, and Reno Orthopedic Group agreed to pay $2.39 million ($815, 794, $971,903, and $ 602, 335 respectively) to settle allegations under the False Claims Act that they bought deeply discounted, re-imported foreign osteoarthritis medication and claimed reimbursement from federal and state health care programs, even though the re-imported medicates were non-reimbursable. Allegedly, the government contended that because the medications were re-imported, their labels allowed for unapproved uses, and there was no manufacturer assurance that the product had not been tampered with or stored inappropriately. The *qui tam* suit was brought by a Senior Musculoskeletal Specialty Manager employed with a manufacturer of one of the allegedly re-imported mediates. The relator will receive $430,000 of the settlement.

Tenet Health Care (N.D. Ga. Oct. 3, 2016)

Tenet Healthcare ("Tenet") and its two Atlanta-based subsidiaries, Atlanta Medical Center and North Fulton Medical Center, will pay over $513 million to settle allegations that it they violated the Anti-Kickback Statute and False Claims Act by paying kickbacks to Hispanic Medical Management so that Hispanic Medical Management would send its pregnant Medicaid beneficiaries to Tenet facilities for their deliveries. Additionally, the government alleged that Tenet told expecting mothers that Medicaid would cover all costs of childbirth if they delivered at a Tenet hospital, leaving them with the false belief that they were unable to select the hospital of their choice. The two subsidiaries were also charged criminally for conspiracy to defraud the U.S. by obstructing the government functions of HHS. Tenet avoided prosecution by engaging in a non-prosecution agreement which required it to cooperate with the government investigation, enhance internal controls and compliance and ethical practices, and further to hire an independent compliance monitor to reduce risk of future violations. TAFEF members Marlan Wilbanks and Susan Gouinlock represented the relator in this case.

www.ingramcontent.com/pod-product-compliance
Lightning Source LLC
Chambersburg PA
CBHW051223200326

41519CB00025B/7230